'We live at an exciting t[...]
part to play in evangel[...]
story to those around us. *Story Bearer* will inspire and equip you to
share your faith in a way that will provoke your friends to explore
the person of Jesus. It is a practical and engaging book that will give
you the confidence and faith to share the good news of Jesus. I wholeheartedly commend it to you. Read it and be inspired!'
The Revd Canon Yemi Adedeji, Director, One People Commission

'Phil is an all-or-nothing-type person and this is clear in his book.
He is a wordsmith who has worked hard crafting these sentences,
paragraphs and chapters to make it so easy to read, apply and live out.'
Dan Blythe, Creative Pastor, Hillsong London

'I've always found telling others about Jesus scary and I've often felt
guilty for not being better at it. This book has been a breath of fresh
air. It is inspiring, hard to put down and simple without being
simplistic, and it makes me think, "I can do this!" Having read it,
I am better equipped to share the news of Jesus and more expectant
about what will happen when I do. I highly recommend it.'
Andy Croft, Senior Pastor, Soul Survivor

'Phil is the ultimate "story bearer". Phil lives in every page, with his
enthusiasm, excitement and passion for stories, and his passion for
people. This book is practical and personal, and has the potential to
equip all of us to discover our story and link it to the story of God.
A great read. I strongly recommend it, well done, friend!'
Roy Crowne, Executive Director, Hope Together

'The world is changed by ordinary Jesus-followers making a difference in their everyday lives. No matter what your experience or
feelings about sharing your faith, this book will inspire you and help
you to do so in a natural and effective way. *Story Bearer* is full of

Phil's contagious passion for Jesus, stories and friendship; it is full of fun and intensely practical, and I am delighted to commend it to you.'
Debra Green, Executive Director, Redeeming Our Communities

'Phil Knox's writing oozes the passion and conviction he lives out in his pursuit of drawing people to Jesus. His punchy style and compelling content will inspire you to want to share your own Jesus story as part of the Big Story with renewed urgency and enthusiasm. Read it and you'll want to live it!'
Simon Guillebaud, Founder, Great Lakes Outreach

'*Story Bearer* is an exceptional book. It is an absolute joy to read, exceptionally written. It will have you laughing and thinking in equal measure! Not only that, but the message it contains is absolutely vital not only for our church but for our nation. It you take this message to heart, it will not only change your world but the worlds of people around you.'
Laura Hancock, Director, Youth for Christ

'Sharing stories is the most significant way you can connect your friends to the life-changing message of Jesus. Furthermore, our research tells us that we are more connected than we think and that our non-Christian friends like us. My friend Phil Knox beautifully unpacks how we can live lives and tell our stories with clarity and confidence. *Story Bearer* will inspire you, encourage you and fill you with hope.'
Dr Rachel Jordan-Wolf, Assistant Director, Hope Together

'A wonderful exploration of the power of the story of Jesus to transform people's lives. Phil is a skilful storyteller and his stories will inspire you and model how you can share your story with others. Immensely practical and equally insightful about why people are

ready to listen to stories, this book will release you from the misconceptions and fears that so often accompany thinking about evangelism. Read this book and start to share!'
John McGinley, Director, Church Planting New Wine, and Development Enabler, Archbishops' College of Evangelists

'The power of story is the heart of our message and vital for mission. Jesus used stories to unlock the hearts of his hearers. Now we are story bearers and this book provides a much-needed resource to harness the power of story for mission in the twenty-first century.'
Dr Andrew Ollerton, Bible Society

'Phil's passion for life and Jesus leaps out of every page of this readable, engaging and helpful book. Filled with personal anecdotes, biblical material and wisdom born of years of experience, this book will encourage people to share their faith in Jesus, whether they are new to the idea or 'old-timers' in need of encouragement. It balances a desire to tell the story of salvation with a pastoral heart, so that it is never coercive but is filled with compassion.'
Canon Dr Andrew Smith, Director of Interfaith Relations for the Bishop of Birmingham

'I wish I had written this book. It has made me laugh out loud in public, filled my eyes with tears, and stoked the fire in me to tell stories of Jesus that captivate and bring hope. *Story Bearer* is exactly what this generation needs to be reading at this time, and the effect it could have on our campuses, in our workplaces and amongst our friends is truly exciting. Please read it, please try it at home, please tell the stories that will come from this. Utterly brilliant.'
Miriam Swaffield, Global Student Mission Leader, Fusion

'People need three things to live: food to eat, a place to live and love, and stories to bear and bare. Phil Knox has written a daringly transparent book on how to live your own story and not someone else's. Discover here the reality that if Jesus is the author (and authority) of your life story, your story is bigger than you. In fact, your story is even big enough, not just to make a difference in the world, but to make a different world.'

Leonard Sweet, bestselling author (*Rings of Fire, Bad Habits of Jesus*), professor and founder of <preachthestory.com>

'Phil is an honest, upfront, in-your-face, passionate follower of Jesus. I love spending time with him. He is a contagious Christian, all or nothing. No mediocre in his world. Fun, loud, creative, breaking the boundaries. This book is a must for you and anyone you know who wants adventure! This book will break you or make you!'

Paul Weston, Pastor, New Generation Church, and Leadership Team, Pioneer

'We all have a story to share, and my good friend Phil Knox gives a brilliant invitation, framework and encouragement for each one of us to find our story in Christ and share it with boldness. His life is an inspiration, and I pray this book inspires many to tell the best story of all – the good news of Jesus Christ, the God who came for our life and freedom.'

Sarah Yardley, Mission and Ministry Lead, Creation Fest

Phil Knox is the head of mission to young adults at the Evangelical Alliance. He has a passion for his generation and the local church, loves learning and has degrees in law and mission and evangelism. Phil is married to Dani and they have two sons, Caleb and Jos. He is an avid runner, enthusiastic waterskier and once broke the world record for the longest five-a-side football match. He is also a performance poet. He lives in Birmingham.

STORY BEARER

STORY BEARER

STORY BEARER

How to share your faith with your friends

Phil Knox

INTER-VARSITY PRESS
36 Causton Street, London SW1P 4ST, England
Email: ivp@ivpbooks.com
Website: www.ivpbooks.com

First published 2020

British Library Cataloguing-in-Publication Data
A catalogue record for this book is available from the British Library.

ISBN: 978–1–78974–155–1
eBook ISBN: 978–1–78974–154–4

Set in Minion Pro 10.25/13.75pt
Typeset in Great Britain by CRB Associates, Potterhanworth, Lincolnshire
Printed in Great Britain by Ashford Colour Press Ltd, Gosport, Hampshire

*Inter-Varsity Press publishes Christian books that are true to the Bible and that
communicate the gospel, develop discipleship and strengthen the church for its mission
in the world.*

*IVP originated within the Inter-Varsity Fellowship, now the Universities and Colleges
Christian Fellowship, a student movement connecting Christian Unions in universities and
colleges throughout Great Britain, and a member movement of the International Fellowship
of Evangelical Students. Website: www.uccf.org.uk. That historic association is maintained,
and all senior IVP staff and committee members subscribe to the UCCF Basis of Faith.*

To my mum and dad, Janet and Martin Knox,
who have borne their stories with such authenticity,
integrity and love that I am one of many whose story
has a different ending.

Contents

Foreword

I am so passionate about seeing everyone in the UK come into a personal relationship with Jesus.

I'm so desperate to see all Christians sharing their faith with those around them.

I'm so energized by the reality that the good news is available to all and should be shared as widely as possible.

I believe that a major move of God is coming to the UK and that it will be driven by a move among his people to share their faith with all those they know.

It's for all these reasons, and many others, that I'm absolutely delighted that my great friend Phil Knox has written *Story Bearer*. This book has the potential to transform our outreach to others, to equip us all to tell our stories more powerfully and to see each one of us released more fully into our God-given mandate to be his witnesses.

We are living in a critical time for our nation and the church. Many of the things people have previously placed their hope in seem to be falling down around them or crumbling before their eyes. Into this vacuum of hope comes the gospel message with profound power. This vital book will help many Christians to begin to have the confidence to take those first steps in sharing their faith with others. It will help each of us to start seeing the places and people with whom we spend most of our time as our very own mission field. We can all begin to realize that in order to discover what it means to be a missionary we simply have to open our front door.

For too long we have often not been prepared to speak to those around us about our first love, and this book practically and simply encourages us and shows us how to do so. In many ways it all starts with a moment of great courage in being prepared to bring our faith into the conversation in the first place. As Christians we need to take ownership for the fact that if people aren't talking about Jesus it's because perhaps we aren't. The world won't start a conversation about a Jesus they've never known, but we can. Our words, deeds and lives can speak so loudly of the Jesus we live for. This book encourages us to do this even more so.

It was Charles Spurgeon who said that 'every Christian is either a missionary or an imposter'. This is a challenge that this book directly takes on. We all need to listen to the wisdom within it, allow the profound challenge to have an impact on our lives, and live differently in our everyday as a result. If the truth in this book is adopted in our lives then it will help us all to avoid any form of 'imposter syndrome' in sharing our faith.

Phil is the real deal. I've known him for many years and have seen him give his life for the sake of the gospel. He lives what he speaks, is generous to those in need and always prepared to give testimony to the faith that drives everything that he is. I am so grateful that he has written this wonderful book and we could all benefit from allowing his words to mould and shape our future witnessing. This is a book for our times. Buy it, read it and live it!

Gavin Calver
Chief Executive Officer, Evangelical Alliance

Preface

In the beginning was the Author.
The answer to the question not yet posed,
Solution to a mystery not yet disclosed,
Liberator to a regime not yet imposed.
There in the background as the story unfolds,
Holding his run from times of old,
Waiting as priests, poets and prophets foretold
Of the Author of all life and love
And all that is good.

Then BANG.
In a moment that is cosmically linkable,
The Author becomes unthinkably shrinkable.
Veiled in flesh the Godhead see.
Hail the incarnate deity.
Because the Author comes down to meet us,
The king of the world becomes a foetus.

And from Judean hills the Story was broadcast
As some logged on, hooked up, tuned in.
And those who did with a wireless connection,
The Author promised life and resurrection.
Weaving tales, leaving trails, breaking jails, removing scales
        from people's eyes
Opened to a kingdom where humanity hails
The Author

But then impaled.
Because love is just words until action prevails,

And this point is proven by blood drawn by nails.
And squaring up sin and death the Author wails,
'IT IS FINISHED.'

But that's just the finale of Season Six,
Because in Season Seven is a box full of tricks.
The Author smashes death in the face with a spade,
Because hell cannot hold his loving tirade.
And for two thousand years the Story continues,
'Get yourself plugged in like you've got nothing to lose.'

So reach for your settings and turn your 'Li-fi' on.
Because the Author is still speaking,
His heart is still beating
And his Story is love and with it he frees us,
Because the Author has a name,
And his name is Jesus.

I've always loved stories: rip-roaring tales of hilarious exploits of embarrassment told in high-school playgrounds; against-all-odds comebacks and adventures from the storyboards of history and sport; myths and fables that draw you close with fatally flawed characters and hit you with a moral sucker punch. As a child I would be repeatedly rebuked for reading Enid Blyton with a torch under the duvet, my activities betrayed by the telltale colourful glow emitted from beneath the blankets . . . 'Just one more chapter . . .'.

This is a book about stories. It's about their power to captivate us, but also their power to communicate ideas, to create and build relationships and ultimately to introduce us to the greatest author of them all, whose bestseller is life itself.

This is a book about relationships. It's about the simple beauty of friendship with another, our need to know and be known, that we were never meant to make it on our own, and the power of relationship to change and transform lives and situations.

And this is a book about good news. It's about the most compelling story in the universe and how we can not only know this for ourselves but also become a story bearer. A story bearer bears and shares the story in such a way that others are caught up in it. And, even better than that, they get to know the Author for themselves.

I was speaking at a Christian festival a couple of years ago. It was my penultimate talk at the end of two weeks away from home. I was missing my family and losing my voice. After preaching your heart out for nine days straight, the last thing you need is some scathing critique from a 15-year-old girl, but as I gathered my Bible and iPad from the stand at the end of the morning meeting I could see her approaching out of the corner of my eye. Lucy was feisty, fiery and angry at the world. Her diminutive size did nothing to make you less scared of her, and she marched towards me before accosting me with a fearsome stare.

'Hiya,' I said, trying to hide my tiredness and fear.

'I want you to know that I wasn't going to come today,' she said.

'Okay,' I said, a little confused.

'I've been here all week but refused to come to the meetings. My friend has been trying to make me come.' At this point, her friend, also called Lucy, popped out from behind her. (It is extremely unhelpful that they both had the same forename for the purpose of storytelling. We shall distinguish them by calling this one 'Christian Lucy'.) I must confess, partly because of the lighting by the stage, I hadn't seen Christian Lucy until this point. Christian Lucy was anything but feisty; she appeared quiet, kind and eager.

'Hiya,' I said to Christian Lucy. I then gave her a little thumbs up to encourage her for dragging non-Christian Lucy along.

'I want you to know', said non-Christian Lucy, 'that I gave up on Christianity a couple of years ago. I'm now a Buddhist.'

'Okay,' I said, wondering where this was going.

'I also want you to know', she continued, 'that God *might* have spoken to me through you this morning.'

'Thanks,' I said, almost asking her to write that down so I could send it on to my boss and my mum as a bit of almost-positive 'customer feedback'.

'Don't try and convert me,' she finished with, 'but I might come back this evening if I feel like it.'

And with that, she marched off to lunch. Christian Lucy turned to look at me apologetically and I was left standing there, not quite sure what had just happened. I decided to pray that afternoon that both Lucys would return that evening and that something amazing might happen in non-Christian, Buddhist Lucy's life. That evening, as the two of them walked through the doors of the venue I thanked God and intensified my prayers for her. The meeting was fairly typical for a youth venue: some singing, a talk and a time of reflection and prayer at the end. As the meeting was coming to a close, there was a captivating sense of calm as 400 teenagers were still and asked God to change their hearts. Then, after about ten minutes someone in the middle of the room started singing. The solo voice beautifully carried the first line, but as it was a well-known worship song, those around her joined in and soon the whole room was singing. The band found the key and we worshipped together in what felt like a heaven-meets-earth moment. After a few more songs I was standing at the back of the venue when I caught a glimpse of some familiar marching feet.

'I want you to know . . .' Here we go again, I thought, but the record had changed: '. . . that God has done the miracle I needed.'

Before I could respond, she continued, 'And it was me who started the singing.' The solo voice that had just led hundreds of other teenagers into soulful song had been hers. 'Anyway, I have to go, I'm leaving the event tonight; my mum is waiting in the car, thanks for everything.'

'Wait a minute, Lucy,' I said. 'Is there not something you need to do before you go home?'

'What?'

'I think you need to tell Jesus you want to follow him again.'

'You're right. I do. What do I say?'

I explained that it should be her words, not mine, but all she had to do was say sorry for going her own way, thank God for loving her and dying for her, and tell him that she trusted him with her life and wanted to do her best to follow him, going his way, not hers, for the rest of her life. She closed her eyes and I winced a little, wondering what was about to come out of her mouth.

'Dear God,' she began, 'I want you to know . . .'

Her prayer was as sincere as a wayward son's who once wrote his speech to his dad from the pigsty. Just as he was, that night she was welcomed home. I love the way the angels throw a party when just one person becomes a Christian.[1] Lucy then headed home.

Very recently I saw Lucy for the first time since this memorable encounter. She is just as feisty but is still following Jesus. She told me about her forthcoming baptism and how she was using that God-given fierce energy to begin a youth club in her town to look out for the vulnerable and lonely teenagers in her community.

The hero of that story is not me. It is not non-Christian Lucy. (Technically, I know now she too, as a result of events, is Christian Lucy. Let's call her Christian Lucy II.) The heroine of our story is Christian Lucy. Without her, Christian Lucy II doesn't get to Jesus. It was her perseverance, her obvious influence, her desire and authenticity that changed the course of her friend's life. The morning after the night that changed Lucy II's life, I had to give one last talk to the festival. I was speaking about the power of relationships. I decided to tell the whole room the story of what had happened in the lives of 'the Lucys' over the past twenty-four hours. When I had finished, I asked Christian Lucy to stand so we could all acknowledge the wonderful way that God had used her. The room erupted with applause. Four hundred of her peers whooped and hollered to congratulate and encourage her.

Preface

This book is written to make us all a bit more like Christian Lucy. In twenty-first-century Britain, religion is deemed increasingly irrelevant and Christians are being squeezed to the periphery of public life. With a diminishing religious identity, people are unlikely to find faith by wandering into a church on a Sunday. Likewise, trust in institutions and people of authority, religious or otherwise, is at an all-time low. Preachers, even if you can get people to listen to them, are unlikely to be the biggest influence in someone becoming a Christian. This is the age of authentic friendship. The most significant factor in someone being introduced to Jesus is a friend, like Christian Lucy. And yet, as Christians, we spend very little time encouraging and equipping each other to be the kind of friends that walk and talk in the way that would help us reach those around us. The task of changing the world is too big and too important to be left to the professionals. My deepest hope as I write this book is that all of us Jesus followers might be more passionate about seeing our friends become Christians, find the challenge less daunting and have the skills to do a few things that will really help our faith-sharing to be as natural and effective as possible. May we all 'be more Lucy'.

Acknowledgments

When you write a book about relationships, it serves as a poignant and timely reminder of how grateful you are for the extraordinary people in your life, whose stories intersect inextricably with your own. Here is a necessarily non-exhaustive list of those I want to show my gratitude to.

With a list like this I am struggling to know where to end, but I know where to begin. Dani, my wife and best friend – thank you for your relentless encouragement and unconditional love.

As you read this book you will discover something of the wonderful family to whom I belong. Mum, Debs, Ste – I am indebted to you for the indelible marks you have made on my storyboard. To the wider Knox and Webb clan, thank you for loving me and allowing me to continue in such a rich family heritage.

I am so thankful to those friends with whom I laugh, cry, struggle and share life. Ads and Beth, Tom and Carys, Rachel and Bob, Andy and Jo, Nathan and Bess, Andy and Laura, Dan and Charlotte, Leon and Debs . . . the list could run and run. Thank you. Because of what you have taught me about friendship, this is your story too.

It takes a village to raise a child and a community to raise a person. I have had the honour for many years of being part of the St Boniface family in Quinton. Thank you for comforting me at the lowest moments and celebrating with me life's victories. Let's keep changing the world together.

I am so grateful for the example and the trust of those who have believed in me. Gavin Calver, Ray Yates, Richard Starkie, Martin Stand, Paul Weston, Neil O'Boyle – this story is a credit to your investment in me.

Acknowledgments

To another astonishing list of people whose beautiful friendship I am also so grateful for: Dave, Jon, Amie, Matt, Paul, Anna, Dan. I hope by reading my story you know the Author better yourselves. His story really is the real deal.

Finally, thanks to Tony and the team at IVP for your encouragement, patience and hard work in publishing *Story Bearer*.

Introduction
There is a story to be told

Have you ever asked a question the response to which elicits way more intrigue and questions than you originally foresaw? It's that feeling that you have somehow unearthed something that taps tenaciously at your curiosity, like having discovered a secret level on a computer game or opened a door to a new house where there is so much to explore. Your question is met with a laugh, a telling grimace or the riposte, 'How long have you got?', and your immediate thought is, 'There is a story that needs to be told.'

Or have you ever known the feeling of having a piece of information, some news, a story even, that is bursting to get out? Worse still, have circumstances prevented you from unleashing this announcement to the world? You feel pregnant with anticipation, knowing that you have in your possession a gift that is everything its recipient could ever want or a weapon that could wreak devastation upon the world of another. I have been the bearer of all kinds of news. I have told stories that have made friends writhe and cry with laughter. I have told a wife that their husband had died. I once told my mum that she was going to be a grandmother.

There are few things more powerful than a story that needs to be told. No wonder there are nearly 300,000 Facebook status updates and 350,000 tweets posted every 60 seconds of every day. We are born storytellers with an inbuilt and innate desire to communicate.

Behind the fabric of the world is a story that holds us together. It is the steel frame upon which the building blocks of life sit. It is the intricate coding behind the programme you see on the screen. It has a hero, a thrilling narrative, a web of relationships, and the plot is still unravelling. It is a comedy, a tragedy, an action film and a love story. It has meaning because it is told by the Creator, the Author of all things. It has direction because it is told by the Way. It is true because it is told by the Truth. It is alive because it is told by the Life. It is dying to be told.

Could it even be that the challenges we face in our world are the result of our having lost sight of this story? The scholar Joseph Campbell stated that all the problems we are experiencing – economic disparity, ecological meltdown, crime, alienation, atomization, war, starvation – are the result of our having no communal myth; a story that unites us, defines us, in relationship to ourselves, other people and nature.[1] We are losing the plot. Literally.

There is a story to be told. And I think deep down we all feel it. That tug on your heart you sense is there because there is a big story on the backstage of life's theatre, there is a grand soundtrack behind the playlist of existence. There is meaning to it all, because life's book has an author, its music has a composer.

And creation is desperate to tell it. Have you ever stood facing a scene of almost excruciating natural beauty? I have stood before mountains and felt microscopic against their towering, majestic presence. I have sat on beaches, experiencing sensory overload as my eyes drink in streams of light reflecting on the water, my ears hearing crash after crash of waves, my nose and mouth full of the taste of salty freshness. I have cradled a newborn son in my arms and known that the love I am able to project is a pale reflection of the love that is held for me.

Paul, an early Christian writer, even said that creation was groaning for the ending of the story.[2] The story has a direction, a trajectory. It is going somewhere. The great invitation of life is to come and join in, to find yourself in the plot.

There is a story to be told. And it is a story that changes lives.

The journey of this book takes place in three parts. In the first, I will begin by making the case that, among the many things that happen to us when we become a Christian, we inherit a new story. We will then go on to consider some of the reasons why we are often so hesitant, impotent even, to share that story with those around us. I will then unpack the power of story and explain why narrative connects so powerfully with us today.

In the second part we will explore four distinct stories that have a role in how we share faith. There are two that need to be told, God's story and your story, and two that need to be listened to, the story of the other and the story of culture.[3] Our preparedness and our ability to tell these stories and our willingness to listen to those around us is an essential starting point if we are to be effective good news people.

Finally, in the third part, we will consider how some of these stories relate to one another and the dynamism that takes place when they collide. At the heart of the interweaving of narratives are relationships, with God and with others. We will explore the power of connection and how we become the best friend we can be. We will consider the importance of our proximity to God, through intertwining our story and his, and look at the relationship between sharing our faith and praying for our friends.

My hope is that by the end of this book you will feel both greater inspiration and greater confidence to be someone who bears a story of great news. I hope that you feel that the word 'evangelism' is more good news to you than bad news. I pray that sharing your faith becomes more natural relationship than nagging responsibility, more genuine delight than guilt-ridden duty.

There are also some practical outworkings; there is some homework to be done. I aim to inspire you to have begun praying for a few people to become Christians by the time you finish reading. I want you to give some thought to what the good news is and how you tell your story so that you are prepared when you get into conversations. To help you with this, there is a host of supplementary material, small-group discussion questions and videos at <www.storybearer.com>.

I hope that by the time you turn the final page, you love God more, love people more, are a better storyteller and a better friend. Let's get started, shall we?

1

Story bearers

You have no idea how different my life is.

As someone who travels around speaking to others about Jesus, I connect with a lot of people and love hearing their stories. Occasionally you get to be part of a big change in their story and, as an evangelist, my favourite change is when someone decides to follow Jesus for the first time. One of the biggest challenges is that, in many encounters, you then leave them to get on with following Jesus on the discipleship journey and rely on others to help them grow beyond this initial point. The inner cynic tells you that their decision will never last.

'Do you remember me?' I was at the foot of the water slide, accompanying my 2-year-old son up the steps for what felt like the fourteen-thousandth time that day. A teenage lad came bounding towards us, excitement in his voice. I scanned my brain database for a name, I dug deep and plumped with about 75 per cent certainty. 'Ben, isn't it?'

I had met Ben two years before, at the same Christian holiday place. I was on the youth team. At the end of a meeting he was sitting on his own and I went to chat with him.

'Are you all right, mate?'

Ben explained that he did not believe in God, but that he was thinking of going into the army and would like me to pray for him that God would protect him. At this point, I would normally pray a really nice prayer of protection, but something made me stop and challenge him.

'God isn't some kind of magic force field, you know,' I explained to a perplexed Ben, who just wanted my comfortable words of blessing. 'He wants to do so much more for you. He wants you to know that you are loved. He wants to forgive you. He wants a relationship with you.'

It is in these moments I often sense God at work, as if something special is about to happen. Even the words that I say here have a boldness and a wisdom that is beyond me. I feel a power surging through my veins.

Ben replied, 'But you have no idea what I have done.' Suddenly, the game had changed. It wasn't that Ben didn't believe in God, but that he thought he had done something so bad that God could never like him, let alone have a relationship with him.

I told Ben that it didn't matter what he had done, how far he thought he was from the Father, how much he had messed up. I told him the story of the prodigal son, how Jesus could not have painted a darker picture of how far the son had fallen in relationship to his dad, and yet the dad was still waiting to welcome him home.

I waited for Ben's response.

He paused for what felt like an eternity before turning to me and saying, 'Okay, I think I am ready to give my life.'

A note at this stage on expectations: evangelism is not normally that easy.

At the bottom of the water slide, I listened to Ben's story two years on. He had abandoned plans to join the army. He wanted instead to become a chaplain in the navy. He was involved in leading worship at his sixth-form Christian Union. He was visibly glowing.

'You have no idea how different my life is.'

We can underestimate the change that takes place when someone becomes a Christian. Paul says, 'If anyone is in Christ, the new creation has come: the old has gone, the new is here!'[1] It is a seismic shift, a complete transformation.

We are forgiven for everything we have ever done wrong.
We enrol as lifelong learners in the way of Jesus.

We receive a place in heaven and have certainty about what happens to us when we die.

We join the mission of bringing heaven to earth.

We become part of the biggest family in the world, with billions of brothers and sisters.

We get a new identity, becoming adopted children of God.

The Spirit of God fills us, comforting us, challenging us and continually making us more like Jesus.

And we have a new narrative. A new story.

To paraphrase St Paul: 'If anyone chooses Jesus, they have a new story, the old chapters have been deleted, the present ones rewritten.' Our story becomes intertwined with God's story. We ask him to take charge of the direction of the plot, we meet new characters who help us on the journey, and we know what the finale will be. Furthermore, we have an increased realization that this story is not just for ourselves. As we get closer to the Author, we hear his heartbeat pounding for those around us. We move from story hearers to story bearers.

On that May day, in that white marquee, the sides flapping in the wind, Ben did not just get his sins forgiven. He became a story bearer. He had no idea how different his life was.

2

Contagious

In 2014 there was an outbreak of the Ebola virus that tragically killed many people, especially in West Africa. The BBC reported the potential threat to the UK at the time and stated: 'The Department of Health said a man had been tested for Ebola in Birmingham but tests for the virus had proved negative.' When a friend sent me the article I immediately knew this, because the man in question was me.

I had just returned from an amazing few days in Abu Dhabi, talking mission with Youth for Christ colleagues from Canada, Singapore, Australia and (crucially to the story) Sierra Leone. After a few days at home I began to feel unwell. Being an all-or-nothing type of person, when I am ill, I like to be properly ill, and a few days after my return from the Middle East I began to feel extremely poorly. My wife Dani was away speaking for the weekend and so I was left in a feverish mess on the sofa watching sports channels. By Saturday lunchtime I was sweating fluids faster than I could consume them, and so I did what any self-respecting thirty-something man would do – I called my mum. She called the medical helpline and in doing so triggered a series of events in which we would witness the breakneck speed of the health-service response when they suspect they have a patient with a dangerous contagious disease. Within an hour I had been quarantined. I was wearing a mask, with a biohazard symbol on my hospital door, feeling like the star of an apocalyptic disaster movie.

I was contained by people who know the power of contagiousness.

As Christians, we have in our heart and in our hands the most contagious message of hope the world has ever known.

The story that we carry should possess us like a virus, captivate our heart like the wildest of romances and dominate our thoughts and actions like the most dangerous addiction. The Christian faith spreads by one person telling another. One of the very first followers of Jesus persuades his friend Nathanael to get involved by inviting him to 'Come and see'. When Jesus leaves his disciples to the global launch party of the church, more than 3,000 join in on day one. In every corner of the world, in every language on the planet, at every time in the last 2,000 years there have been story bearers who have told that story to others. And as a result, others have bought in and joined the family. When you speak to most Jesus followers and ask them about the important steps on their journey, it will involve someone telling them the story.

The Christian story should be the most contagious thing in the universe.

As I sat in that hospital room and feverishly sweated effortlessly through another set of clothes before the inevitable chills, I felt the constrictive mask around my mouth. I became aware of the sterile conditions that I occupied and in a lonely way remembered that I had not been seen by anyone in hours. The introduction of barriers can stop things from spreading. Put another way, the conditions must be right for contagiousness. You can do things to yourself and others can do things to you to stop you passing something on. It seems to me that this is true of so many Christian story bearers. These are the main reasons why the most contagious story in the world does not spread. Let's explore some of these and, as we do, ask yourself whether any of them are true for you and what you might do to overcome them.

Proximity: the story bearer lacks any meaningful contact with people who need to hear the story

For disease to spread, proximity is crucial. You have to be close to someone. It is a commonly held belief that it is better to have chicken pox when you are young as the symptoms are more bearable as a child than as an adult. So a common occurrence in the lives of toddlers is the 'Pox Party' where healthy children are encouraged to hang out with, hug and, in extreme cases, rub against infected children in the hope that they might develop red spots. If Christians do not have friends who are not Christians whom they regularly spend time with, it is unlikely that they will be able to pass on the story. Do you have friends who aren't yet Christians? Are you close to them? Do you spend enough time with them for the story to spread?

Potency: the story bearer does not trust the power of the story

There are a few types of salesperson. The first is the one who will say anything to get you to buy the product they are selling, to the extent that you are not sure whether they believe in what they are selling or not. These are my least favourite. Then there are the kind who genuinely believe in what they are selling and ooze enthusiasm for not just the product but the whole field they are in. These are the best kind and probably the most effective. Then there is the reluctant salesperson. Their heart is not in it, they don't like the product and it could even be that they have never even tried it. And you can tell.

There are some Christians like this. They are not sure that the story could have an impact on their friend's life, or if it even works in theirs any more. Their relationship with the Author is so distant that even if their friend was looking for him, they might not know where to point or whether it would be worth their while. Is Jesus the most important person in your life? Is following him your first priority? Do you really believe that if your friends encountered him it would completely change their lives, or would it just slightly improve them?

Desire: the story bearer does not want to share the story

At this point, the infection analogy falls short. With my virus in that hospital bed, I could not simply choose not to be contagious. When it comes to sharing the story, however, if there is no desire on the part of the story bearer to share it, it is unlikely to travel. Many stories are

6

untold because the teller wants them to remain so. My own reluctance comes from three places.

Embarrassment. I like to be liked. I would go further: I love to be loved. I have felt the rush of adrenaline when I sense approval, affirmation and admiration, especially when I meet new people and there is an instant click. I was on a university pub crawl with some new-found friends. Conversation was flowing, interests exchanged, jokes, laughter. I was at the centre of it all, feeling the God-given rush of relational exchange. Then this guy chips in:

'There's this girl on my corridor who is one of those Christians. Like one of those militant, awful ones. She's a nightmare.'

Laughter.

Apart from me. Part of the art of connecting with someone is finding common ground. When it is clear that not only is the ground uncommon, it is offensive to the other, pushing back against the grain can feel instantly unpopular. I have been in many situations like this over the years and when I think of them I remember as much shame in not standing up and making the most of the opportunity as I do pride for overcoming my embarrassment and speaking up to go against the grain.

Fear. Friendship is precious. And, like many precious things, it can also be extremely fragile. You do not toss Ming vases around like rugby balls. There have been many occasions with good friends where I have not wanted to take a conversation down a certain road, because I know that its destination is a disagreement of views or an opportunity to share a story I don't want to. I am afraid that my storytelling will make things uncomfortable and awkward, and that the casualty will be my relationship with my friend, or at least it will be a backward step. I have friends who have kept me at arm's length having found out I am a Christian and after I'd engaged them in conversation about faith.

7

Uncertainty. On 8 May 2006, Guy Goma, a business studies graduate, walked into BBC Television Centre in West London to interview for a job as a data cleanser. At the same time, Guy Kewney, a technology expert, walked into the same building to make a television appearance commenting on a news story. Mr Kewney was left in reception and, in the most hilarious case of mistaken identity, Mr Goma suddenly found himself on a sofa opposite a news anchor with three live TV cameras pointing at him. He was asked questions on a subject he knew nothing about.

I have often felt like Guy Goma when in conversations with people about my faith, sometimes to the extent that I feel like I am doing more harm than good.[1] I am afraid I will be stumped by a question, say something offensive or humiliate myself by mumbling a fudged answer with misquotes, exaggerations and contradictions. I can feel that unless I answer perfectly, with charisma and conviction, my friend will write off my faith and never want to explore what it means to be a Christian. My fear of not knowing what to say has meant that I have bottled opportunities to go deeper in conversation and increased my reluctance to be contagious.

Opportunity: the story bearer lacks meaningful chances to pass on the story

Every day we abide by many of the unwritten rules of our society. Starting a conversation with people on public transport is met with a suspicious glance that says, 'What on earth do you think you are doing?' Overtaking people in a queue without invitation rarely results in intervention from fellow queue members, but extreme eye rolling and whispers of, 'How rude!' Etiquette demands that we control certain bodily functions in public places.

A few of these unwritten rules act as containment measures for the story by controlling infectious opportunities. The first of these is busyness. A woman once moved to New York city from another culture and, having been there a short amount of time, began introducing herself to others with the words, 'Hello, I'm Busy.' So engrained in our culture is constant activity as a badge of honour that this woman thought these words were a traditional American greeting.[2] Balancing work or education, family, hobbies, church, relaxation, exercise, email, entertainment, sleep and friends is exhausting, and that is before you have invested valuable time making sure you have kept the world updated through social media and kept tabs on how everyone else is doing. Finding time in the midst of that to share the story can be a challenge.

The second rule is that your lifestyle and views conform to a certain minimum standard of social acceptableness. Society's views on all sorts of issues change over time and Christians find themselves out of sync. A lifestyle that is distinctively different from the trajectory of society will create intrigue and opportunity for the story to be told. However, the pressure to conform, to only voice opinions that are inoffensive to the prevailing values of the time, to separate a private faith from a public life, will make opportunities of story sharing rare.

So we have these two powerful factors in play. The contagiousness of the story versus the forces of containment. This is the backdrop against which this book is set. This book is about tipping the balance in favour of contagiousness and harnessing the power of relationship and narrative to unleash the story.

If you were interested, I didn't have Ebola or anything very sinister at all. It was just a really bad case of man flu.

3

The power of story

Story is atomic. It is perpetual energy and can power a city. Story is the one thing that can hold a human being's attention for hours.[1]
(Donald Miller)

Words: the building blocks of stories

Words have power. I remember being teased at school. I was short, squeaky and had sticky-out ears. Funnily enough, these features were highlighted from time to time by others at an age when you haven't got a solid enough identity for them not to mean anything. With a bruised self-esteem, I would often go home and tell my parents. I remember their words as much as those of the teasers. They told me that good things came in small packages, to consider how valuable tiny jewels were, that God loved me the way I was, and that 'sticks and stones may break my bones, but words could never hurt me'. I understand why they gave me the last piece of advice; that I could shrug off hurtful words in a way I would not be able to if it were rock being used to pummel my head. I comprehend the sentiment of the statement. But the reality is that words can cause harmful and lifelong injuries that cut deeper and heal slower than sticks and stones.

Words have extreme potency to build up, encourage and inspire or to devastate, derail and destroy. Sadly, we will all know friends who have listened to negative voices in their life and believed them, sometimes with terrible consequences. In my grandfather's class at school was a boy who was bullied for being overweight. He was called 'fatty' and constantly compared to a pig. One day he tragically decided to take his own life. Sticks and stones may break my bones, but words can sometimes do even worse things.

But they can also do the opposite.

At school, I enjoyed learning, but have always been easily distracted and prone to over-confidence. That combination was not very helpful when revising for exams, and my parents, particularly my dad, would put a great deal of pressure on me to do well at school. He was an extremely successful lawyer and had achieved his success through huge amounts of hard work, so during exam periods would try to cajole me into doing the same. I needed it. However, on the last morning of my last A-level exam there was a letter addressed to me, in his handwriting, on my bedside table with my morning coffee. The letter said many things, but these words I see as clearly embossed in my mind's eye today as they were on the page in 2001: 'Phil, I know I have put pressure on you to do well in your exams, but I want you to know that I will not love you any more if you do well, or love you any less if you do badly.' Eighteen years on those words still mean a great deal. Words are powerful.

Words can completely change situations: 'Will you marry me?' 'I'm pregnant.' 'They think it's cancer.' 'Let there be light.' In fact, if you were looking for ultimate proof of the power of words, the universe was literally spoken into being. The opening verses of the Bible show God speaking life, creating the heavens and earth by uttering syllables from his mouth. Words create new realities. Use them wisely.

Words are the building blocks of stories.

Mind-blowing: what stories do to our brains

If you are ever in a social situation and are looking for a question to get people talking, ask a group of any age what television programmes they watched when they were growing up. This question has the power to animate the most passive character and can result in quite a heated discussion. Within minutes you may find you have intelligent, articulate people in passionate debate about who would win in a fight between Wonderwoman and the Thundercats, humming the Teenage Mutant Ninja Turtles theme song and boasting about the size of their Star Wars action figure collection. We remember our childhood cartoons, the books we read and the made-up stories from our parents' head. And we do so for very good scientific reasons.

Your brain is an incredibly complex organ, and in recent years brain scans have been able to watch the way the brain reacts to certain stimuli. Among them have been stories. The brain has been scanned while it has been listening to a story. And what happens is remarkable.[2]

When listening to a story, three significant chemicals are released in your brain. The first is cortisol. Cortisol acts to lock in your attention to what is going on and helps memories to form. It helps create what is known as a 'flashbulb memory', a vivid and detailed snapshot of a moment in time that can stay with you for a lifetime. The reason you can remember exactly where you were or what you were doing when you heard a piece of significant news is the result of a flashbulb memory like this.

The second dispatch from your brain is oxytocin. Oxytocin is best known for its role in childbirth, helping the birth process, breast-milk production and creating a natural bond between baby and mother. It is these emotional properties that compel the listener of a story. Have you ever wondered why, when watching a film or reading a book, you feel so desperate that a certain outcome occurs or a particular character succeeds, even though it will have no effect whatsoever on you? That is oxytocin doing its work, aligning your heart with that of the character, creating empathetic links that put you in their shoes and planting you temporarily in their story.

We all love it when a story results in a happy ending, and our physiological response contributes to our enjoyment. This is where the third substance, dopamine, comes into play. Dopamine is a pleasure chemical. It makes us feel good. It is released when you succeed, smoke, take recreational drugs and spend time on social media. It is also addictive. The reason you walk out of a cinema with a deep sense of satisfaction and why the final page of a novel brings a smile to your face is the dopamine swirling around your brain.

Research into the power of story has gone further. In a study into the science of storytelling, neurologists scanned not just the brains of people listening to stories, but also those of the people telling the stories. The findings were extraordinary. They found that brain activity was mirrored in the teller's brain and the hearer's, that the same chemical patterns emerged at exactly the same time as the story was told.[3] Something profound happens when you tell a story that connects you to the person you are telling it to. You might say that you sync your brain with theirs.

We are fearfully and wonderfully made.

It's as if we were created by an Author who loved stories.

It's as if Jesus knew what he was doing when he used stories to communicate the deepest truths of divinity and humanity.

Digital: the power of story today

The biological reasons why stories work are just the beginning. There is a significant rationale for why using stories to communicate truth is not just timeless, but timely in today's society and culture. Something has changed for us as a human race in the last thirty years. There has been a seismic shift.

If you were cryogenically frozen in 1972 and have just woken up, if you are an inhabitant of a small Amazonian tribe or have made a vow of technological purity for religious reasons, for the purposes of this next section you will need to do some research about the internet, the digital age and mobile technology. For the rest of us, I am going to assume that you have noticed some changes in the last few years or you have grown up in a world where Google is a verb, computers have always been small enough and your mobile phone is nothing short of an additional limb. Few would dispute that a digital revolution has taken place, but many are oblivious to the depth and breadth of its impact. A limitless, digital world affects our lives in all sorts of ways, from how we spend our time to the nature of forming and maintaining relationships, from our attention spans to our access to mildly amusing videos of cats dressed as superheroes. But perhaps the most underestimated and pervasive change has come in the way we access information, and it has massive implications for how we communicate and how we learn.

First, let us consider the abundance of information available to us. I was fourteen years old. It was the last day before the Easter holidays began. As you went into the last lesson of each subject before a holiday period you crossed fingers, toes and limbs and joined with your peers in communal prayers that no holiday project would be commissioned. My RE teacher, Mr Collins, would never oblige: 'Your project for the holidays is "The Life of Martin Luther King".' Cue communal groans followed by sackcloth and ashes, weeping and gnashing of teeth. Being back in the dark ages of research, and not being that one kid in my class with Microsoft Encarta on my computer, my first port of call was a trip to the library and an appointment with *Encyclopaedia Britannica* in the reference section.

I realize that readers born after 1990 are reading this with disbelief, pity or scorn, but I assure them it is true.

The history of *Encyclopaedia Britannica* is illustrative of the pace of growth of information availability. In 1771 it had one editor, three volumes, and in 2,500 words summed up all you needed to know about a civilized world. Less than 100 years later, in 1860, there were 18,000 pages of knowledge. The versions that I would be thumbing through in 1997 on the way to the Martin Luther King entry would be over 30 volumes constructed by over 10,000 contributors.[4] Today, this once legendary bastion of information pales into utter insignificance, its ramparts laid to ruin by the marauding, unstoppable armies of the digital revolution. Over 10 articles are edited on Wikipedia every second and, on average, 700 new items are added each day.[5] We have at our thumb tips more information in a matter of milliseconds than our grandparents had access to in their entire lifetimes. If information is power, then we are all intergalactic emperors.

Second, and more pertinently, let us reflect on the journey to information. As I researched my Easter project, the journey was a linear one. I found the pages in the book, turned them sequentially and read from left to right. This journey can be traced back to a Mr Gutenberg.

In the fifteenth century, Johannes Gutenberg stopped crushing apples and used his press instead to make books. The fruit (pun intended) of this innovation was the printing press, and it would have an impact on the way in which humanity accessed information for centuries. Access for everyone was accelerated, pages and pages of books and manuscripts were produced. And when you read a book, or words written on a piece of paper, those words reinforce a linear narrative; you read one word after another in a straightforward manner, and the pages turn numerically in order.

This stimulates a certain part of our brains.

When we compare and contrast this pathway to the glistening new tarmac of the information superhighway, we find a completely different non-linear journey. When you type words into a search engine, you enter a matrix of web pages, videos and images, multiple tabs, media and platforms. The journey is as full of back arrows, hyperlinks and new windows as it is of page turns. The way we read a web page is completely different from the way we read text on a page. Heat maps from studies into where eyes look on a screen show that after being initially drawn to the top right-hand corner, they will scan down the page as much as across it. We are no longer in linear Kansas, this is non-linear Oz. Gutenberg is dead; long live King Google.

This stimulates a different part of our brains.

Some years ago someone showed me a brain. A real one. A dead one. They pulled it out of a jar and held it aloft with pride like some kind of dark, anatomical opening to *The Lion King*. They explained that every human brain has two halves and that each half operates in an entirely different way from the other. In a brief, crude neurological summary, the left hemisphere of the brain processes information in a more linear fashion and is more logical, rational and analytical. It is better at maths. The right side of the brain is more artist than accountant, more theatre than news channel, more suited to creativity, metaphor, image and abstract thought. It is better at art.[6]

The digital revolution has led to an awakening of the right brain in terms of the way we access information. Neurologists are finding that the brains of young people are even being wired differently from those of previous generations. But what does any of this have to do with stories?

Stories stimulate the right side of the brain.

In today's world, we can thank internet engagement and embrace technological change for increasing an openness to story as a means of communication. Put another way, if we are to connect with contemporary society we must use right-brain media: poetry, music, images, video, art . . . and stories.

Pervasive: stories are everywhere

Fascinatingly, we see this being worked out in many of the spheres of influence in our world. An hour on YouTube watching music videos will show you the prevalence of story in popular artists' expressions of their songs. Very few merely show the band playing the song; instead a narrative unfolds during the verses, with characters, a plot and an ending. Often the artist will insert themselves into the story, perhaps to tell their own tale of recent life events or state of mind.

As social media evolves, a significant development has been the movement by many platforms inviting users not just to capture a moment in time but to use a sequence of photos, statuses or events to tell a story. And young people are embracing it in their droves, telling their own Insta, Snapchat or Facebook stories to their audiences of friends, fans and followers.

The cold, clinical world of corporate boardrooms is also far from exempt. The business consultant and author Paul Smith describes the shift taking place in sales teams and executives, in boardrooms and factories, towards the use of story in internal and external communications.[7] At Nike, the sportswear company, each of their senior executives has a full-time professional storyteller assigned to them to assist them in not just capturing stories from across the world of the impact the brand has on athletes and communities but also coaching them in becoming better storytellers themselves.

There has never been a better time to embrace the power of story.

And breathe . . .

So far, we have explored three key ideas that are central to this book. First, we have walked together through a white marquee with Ben and described the change that happens when someone becomes a Christian, that among a range of transformations they begin to bear a story. Second, we have spent time in a hospital room considering the contagious nature of the Christian faith and asked why its spreading might be inhibited. Third, we have dabbled in neurology, history and business to explore how stories work across numerous landscapes and why they might be our greatest tool in evangelism.

We turn now to four storylines. As we read about them, I want you to picture each of them as a thread, important in its own right and worth studying, knowing and learning more of. As each new thread is introduced, we will weave it into the others and consider the connection points between them. So sit back, take a sip of your favourite hot beverage and let me tell you a story.

4

God's story

Welcome to the first of our stories. In this chapter I will take you on a walk through the pages of the Bible from Genesis to Revelation. My main aim is to give you a 'view from the balcony', to give you enough detail that you appreciate the richness and length of the story, but keep it short enough that you can see the big overarching themes. On the journey, I have tried to arrange stops at all the major landmarks and I have included a few illustrative stories of my own to reinforce key themes. I hope that this chapter helps you zoom out to see the big Bible picture and serves like that moment when you are doing a jigsaw and you join a few pieces that initially you did not realize fitted so closely together. Welcome to the greatest story the world has ever known.

Beginnings

Life is about connections. I find the moment two people meet for the first time interesting. The meeting of eyes, the chink of a glass, the handshake, the slight raising of the head – 'All right?' – or the straight-in-for-the-hug. What might their relationship become? Will it be a one-time meeting, or will they go on to be best of friends and share many memories together?

I love meeting people. I'm fascinated by people's lives, their journeys and what has made them into the complex bundle of gifts, memories, emotions and characteristics they are today. We were created to connect, to co-star on the storyboard of one another's lives and for the circles of our lives to intersect with the circles of others. Human beings may be more truly described as 'human relatings'. There is, within all of us, a deep desire to know and be known.

We are like this because we are made in the image of God. This is a God who doesn't just love relationships, didn't just create relationships, but a God who is even in relationship with himself. For as long as people have been calling themselves Christians, they have been exploring how to relate to a God who is one and at the same time a God who is three persons. It is even more interesting to consider how these three persons might relate to one another; indeed the early church fathers, when attempting to describe this divine mystery of the Trinity, began to use the word 'perichoresis'. It has come to mean 'interpenetration', and the image conjured by these linguistic gymnastics is that of a dance.[1]

When I think of dancing, I have a number of instinctive reactions. The first is the beginning of a cold sweat as I start to think of being made to hold a girl's hand during country dancing as a 9-year-old. I next think of the pure joy of expression of throwing all kinds of shapes in student night clubs, and finally land on the Latin and ballroom lessons I took with my wife a couple of years ago. The incredibly patient Dani's bruised feet bear witness to the fact that I was a slow learner but the abiding memories from those nights in the dingy social club are extreme intimacy. The feeling of holding someone so close and moving with her was dynamic and intimate. I am not surprised in the slightest that so many partners on *Strictly Come Dancing* end up in a relationship with one another! And I am also not surprised that this is the image that theologians have used to describe the interrelationship of Father, Son and Holy Spirit, that the three can be found in the blur of movement of extreme, dynamic intimacy.

In the beginning God created the heavens and the earth.

On the dance floor of history, this disco deity has always been in motion. The story of God begins here. His initial existence precedes his innovative expression. Before he is creative, he is constant. Before

20

sunsets and selfies, baboons and Bieber, horses, chestnuts and horse chestnuts, God is.

God is.

He is there before the story begins, like an author with his fingers hovering over the keyboard, a blank page in front of him.

And out of the overflow of this relationship of Father, Son and Holy Spirit comes a yearning for relationship. God is love and God is constantly seeking an object for his affection.

In the beginning God created the heavens and the earth.

This is the beginning of the story of God. Without his story we don't have a story.

So God creates. And he saves the best until last. We are the pinnacle of God's creation.

Some years ago, as a young adult, in the run-up to Christmas I nostalgically reflected on how the magic of Christmas had been eroded in my late teens. Determined to recapture some of the mystery and anticipation, I asked my loved ones to surprise me with something fun rather than functional that I could play with on Christmas Day. As I woke and made my bleary-eyed way to the tree on Christmas morning I was delighted to have the biggest box to open, and as the mountains of wrapping paper began to grow, the sound of Mariah and Slade in the air, I tore off the wrapping paper to reveal the most magnificent Lego castle I had ever seen. My day was set. Interrupted only by church and a plateful of turkey and roast potatoes, I built obsessively and enthusiastically as my family talked, played games and watched the Queen and Poirot around me. As the fire died down, people were going to bed and the clock was ticking towards midnight as I placed the last knight behind the last cannon on the last battlement of the last tower. I stood back with the kind of deep sense of satisfaction I imagine Michelangelo had, having left his last brushstroke on the Sistine Chapel, or David Beckham had as the ball hit the net to send England to the 2002 World Cup, or One Direction had as they penned the last note of 'What Makes You Beautiful'. It felt like, to date, the best thing I had ever made (my two sons probably now take that accolade). I imagine it is with this kind of satisfaction that God stood back and observed his craftsmanship in humanity.

So our story begins, and it is in perfect step with God's story – Creator and creation in sync. This is how it was meant to be. Our forebears walk with God in the cool of the day.

A cosmic break-up

But this connection made in heaven does not last long. The Bible's opening chapters portray paradise created and lost; our ancestors famously make some bad fruit choices. At its core (note the second fruit-based pun of the book so far) is disobedience, rebellion and a lack of trust in the Creator. And like a virus it invades our hearts and is passed from generation to generation.

It had been the perfect day so far. The fairy-tale wedding of Sara to Sergeant Jamie Huxley had been the sort that not only moved grandmothers to tears as can be expected, but also left a few of the groom's commanding officers apologetically dabbing their eyes and trying to hold their 'stiff upper lip' steady. Sara had come through a life-threatening illness, while her childhood sweetheart Jamie had suffered terrible burns to the right side of his body when a roadside bomb had hit his unit's vehicle, from which he emerged the lone survivor. After a guard of honour and a ride in the wedding car, a superb Aston Martin DB7, back to the house, they were waiting to emerge to their expectant guests at the wedding breakfast in an immaculate marquee. The marquee sat in a picturesque setting in the Oxfordshire village, meticulous thought and preparation given to the interior design, with lilies lining the walls, a stage at one end and the most glorious chocolate fountain next to the archway through which the guests had arrived.

'Stop it, girls, they are about to arrive.' Sara's sisters, bridesmaids Katie and Francesca, aged six and eight respectively, had been well behaved throughout the service, quietened by sweets and the promise of TV between the service and reception, but now the sugar had hyped them up and the TV had been turned off. Francesca had torn emotions during the day, having developed a special bond with her big sister during her illness, but felt jealous of Jamie taking her away. As the guests were invited to turn their eyes to the door to welcome the happy couple, the two young girls were engaged in a fight for the remote control, which their mother, also trying to take photographs, was struggling to control.

'My lords, ladies and gentlemen, the bride and groom . . .' As applause erupted and the marquee flap was pulled back, Katie and Francesca escaped their mother's attention and moved obliviously towards the door upon which everyone's anticipatory gaze was set. Katie managed to get two hands on to the remote that Francesca held. With a defiant tug, Francesca pulled away, but her excess momentum sent her reeling backwards. As the beaming couple emerged into the tent there was a blur of pink as Francesca tumbled into the adjacent table, a crashing sound and that terrible moment when time stands still and then plays in slow motion. The item most in motion was the chocolate fountain, which landed at the couple's feet, jets of molten brown liquid splattering their faces, Jamie's pristine regimental uniform and Sara's white dress. As time seemed to return to normal speed, guests ran to the couple to try to help, Sara took one look at her dress and began to weep, and no-one knew quite what to say or do. Only Katie noticed her sister frantically pressing a button on the remote control she was holding through hot, angry tears: 'Francesca, what are you doing?'

The young bridesmaid looked up and said, 'I want to rewind.'

From the moment we messed up as a human race, the cry of our story has been, 'We want to rewind.' We know that all is not well between us and God. 'The heart of the human problem is the problem of the human heart.'[2] When a relationship turns sour, when you fall out with a friend, it can feel like there is a barrier between the two of you. So it is with our story and God's. We want to go back, to wipe the slate clean, to rewind the story.

But God's story has a cry as well. He is in hot pursuit of relationship with his creation.

Some years ago there was an earthquake in Turkey. At 2.04 pm it ripped through a village, flattening homes, shops, coffee houses and restaurants. In the aftermath, it was chaos as survivors searched for their loved ones. Through the crowds, one man emerges, panic on his bearded face, running towards the place where he had dropped his son to school that morning. Imagine the terror in his eyes as he turns a corner and sees the flattened remains of the school, where previously classrooms had stood. Through the noise of confused shouting and wails he begins to call the name of his son, 'Armand, Armand, Armand . . .'. With little deliberation or plan, he starts to search through the remains, tossing aside loose bricks, 'Armand, Armand, Armand . . .'. As the noise dies down, other fear-filled parents observe him, trying to persuade him of the futility of his efforts. 'Either leave me alone or join me and help me,' he replies with determination. 'I am going to find my son – 'Armand, Armand, Armand . . .'. As night falls, he carries on relentlessly, his muscles burning, the skin on his hands wearing thin, his vision blurry, his nostrils full of the smell of brick dust and fumes, 'Armand, Armand, Armand . . .'. His voice becomes increasingly hoarse, at times down to a whisper as 12 hours pass, 24 hours, 36 hours. At near exhaustion, 47 hours in, the father uncovers a wooden door and flips it over, revealing a cavity in the rubble. As the dust settles he looks down, his gaze greeted by two pairs of eyes. One pair of eyes turns to the other pair of eyes and says, 'You see, I told you my daddy would come.'

Pursuit

Since the beginning of time, God has pursued us. His intrinsic desire to be in relationship is insatiable and his story is one of him trying to find ways to be with his creation. But the seemingly inescapable barrier is that we are wayward and wanton, as lost as a penguin in the Sahara. If the story was just told from our point of view it would reek of forgetfulness, careless mistakes and at times downright defiance. But from God's perspective, he is like the patient parent who will wait for their children to pick themselves up and get back on the bike. He is like the husband or wife who, though wronged and mistreated, is waiting to give their spouse one more chance. And his story, as revealed in the Bible, shows us an author who, one way or another, will bridge the gap between himself and those he loves. Because when you are in love you will do anything to be with that person.

I sat in the driver's seat and the blood drained from my cheeks, rendering my face a ghostly white. The smell of brickwork and saw-dust filled my nostrils. I tried to stay calm and turned the radio off. Questions flashed through my mind. Had I killed anyone? Would I ever be allowed to drive again? What would my mum say? It was her car and I had driven it into my girlfriend's house. I knocked on the door and said the most obvious thing. 'Dani, I've just driven my car into your house.'

It was an expensive mistake and one of the most embarrassing experiences of my life, made worse by the fact that there were builders on scaffolding a few doors down who were already giddy with excitement at the prospect of telling the story that night at the pub. I had been away and not seen Dani for a few days. Time was short and, as I drove my mum's massive automatic Volvo estate round to see her, all I could think of was the moment that would take place in a few seconds' time when I would see her face. Impatient, I swung around the corner a little bit too fast, which probably would have been fine had I pressed the right pedal next. My mum's Volvo was a little unfamiliar to me and I missed the brake pedal by a good few centimetres and landed on the accelerator instead. The car plunged into the house.

When you are in love you will do anything to be with that person.

The journey we are about to embark on is a tour of the landmarks of God's efforts to find a way to be with his people and overcome the relational barriers. As we do so, the paradigm of story is a helpful one, especially when understanding the Bible, because when an author sets out to pen a narrative, he or she knows where it is headed. There is an arc, a destination; the author knows how the story ends before beginning it, and the roles the characters will play. When it seems that one means of relating to humanity is not working out in God's original intention, God is not like a surprised inventor, forced to go back to a heavenly drawing board to work on Plan B. God's story is always pointing forward to something, or someone, to come. From that moment of initial disobedient rebellion, what happens next?

Reboot

Adam and Eve have children and the earth is populated, but the spirit of rebellion in their descendants is alive and well. Wickedness covers the earth. Facing the pain of a creation out of sync with its creator, God applies the logic of a twenty-first-century human who has a computer problem and decides to turn it off and on again. The one remaining character in the reboot is a faithful, good man called Noah. He builds a big boat and the story starts again.

Our next stop is a nomadic, tent-living farmer called Abram for some significant foundations to be laid in God's story. God chooses Abram, changes his name and tells him at the ripe old age of ninety-nine that not only is he going to be a dad, but that members of his family line will be an uncountable number. He has a son called Isaac, who has a son called Jacob, who has a few sons, one of whom is a young dreamer with a famous coat called Joseph (the son, not the coat). Joseph saves his family from famine by gaining favour with the Egyptian royal family, and Team Jacob move to Egypt and become so numerous and influential that they become a threat.

The next passenger on our biblical tour bus is Moses, a messed-up kid supposed to have been killed at birth, but who escapes via a basket down a river to be rescued by an Egyptian princess and raised in dual heritage. His identity is further confused when he kills a man, flees to neighbouring Midian and marries into a third culture. It is no wonder he is the first person in the Bible to ask, 'Who am I?' After an encounter with God and the small matter of moving 600,000 men (women and children probably tip this over 1 million) across the Egyptian border, via a sea that splits in half, Moses is instrumental in setting up the rules of engagement through which God will relate to his people for the next few hundred years.

The deal is that God wants his people to be different, set apart, so that they can not only have the best lives for themselves, but they can show the rest of the world what God is like. So God's story outlines both the broad brushstrokes of expected human behaviour ('You shall not murder, commit adultery, steal etc.') but also zooms into the intricate detail of daily life (what animals are acceptable to eat, keeping clean, and coping with mould).

Central to this part of the story is not only how God's people will maintain relationship with one another, but how they will stay right with God and cope with their wayward hearts and actions. A sacrificial system is set up through which the people understand that their sin is dealt with through the ritual slaughter of animals, and they thank God for the good things he gives by sacrificing the first portion of their harvest back to him. The overarching principle of this arrangement, or covenant, is that if the people obey God and stay right with him, through faith demonstrated by obeying the rules, then all will go well for them; they will live where they are meant to and be protected from their enemies. If they do not trust God, choose to disobey him, mistreat each other and act like everybody else around them, there are disastrous consequences.

Remember

We next stop at some careless forgetfulness. My dad used to tell me that I would forget my head if it was not screwed on, but I am in good company. In 2016 a Brazilian man forgot his wife and left her at a service station, driving sixty miles before realizing she was missing. As you can imagine, she was rather angry with him when he sheepishly returned. We are a forgetful people and we need things to remind us about the important things in life. The next chapter of God's story begins with some astonishing forgetfulness. The people of God have escaped slavery, trudged around a desert, fought tooth and nail to take possession of the land God has for them, and then the reader of the story is met with these words: 'After that whole generation had been gathered to their ancestors, another generation grew up who knew neither the LORD nor what he had done for Israel.'[3]

Within a generation they have forgotten the most important moments of their tribe's history. We are forgetful people. This is surely why God keeps giving us ways to remember the story. The people of God would tie the commands of God to their hands and foreheads. Even before they had left Egypt, God was telling them how they were going to remember this victorious moment in the years to come by eating the very meal from that night in a deeply experiential way that connected all five senses. Today, millions of Christians across the world will eat bread and drink wine to remember a different story, to connect with it and to find their place in it once more.

Despite their forgetfulness, God has not given up the chase and in this next instalment of the pursuit raises up chosen leaders, known as judges, to reconnect with his people and their story. The judges have some eye-watering adventures involving swords disappearing into obese men's stomachs, tent pegs driven into army commanders' heads and the better-known victories of little Gideon and shaggy-haired Samson.

As the nation of Israel develops, God reluctantly agrees to let them have a king, and Saul falls in and then out of favour to tee up the glory years of the people of God under King David. After defeating Goliath and spending ten years on the run, the song-writer, harp-player, battle-winner and occasional adulterer and murderer becomes the kingdom's greatest king. Israel seems set for years of prosperity and favour.

But by the time David's grandson is on the throne, the people and their leader have forgotten the story, its guiding principles and the consequences of rebellion against God. The kingdom that David ruled splits in two, with Israel in the north and Judah in the south, and each has its own lineage of kings. These kings vary wildly in their godliness, with some pushing boundaries of evil to extraordinary lengths and others humbly dragging their nation back in line. The pendulum of obedience to rebellion swings one way then the next, with prophets persistently insisting on Godly living and warning of the dire consequences of national rebellion. These same prophets are also doing something else. They look forward to a new day, a new kingdom, brought in by a different kind of king. When you sift through the writings of bleak and imminent judgment there are quiet hints of someone coming, whispers of hope.

Before we get to that stop on the tour, things have to get worse before they can get better. Without the protection and blessing of God, invading armies eventually have their way, with much of the Israelite population being captured and taken into exile in Babylon. Leaders like Daniel demonstrate living faithfully when inhabiting a foreign land, and Nehemiah tells his own story of returning from exile, home to Jerusalem, to rebuild the walls and try to reboot the story once more.

And then, 400 years of silence. Between the books of Malachi and Matthew, nothing. The people of God are occupied by competing empires and passed like a war trophy from one civilization to the next. From the Babylonians to the Persians, from the Persians to the Greeks and from the Greeks to the Romans. And under Roman rule, at the time of a Roman census, a baby is born.

The hero

I remember the first time I watched a James Bond film. For two hours I was transfixed by Sean Connery in *From Russia with Love*. Bond's appeal for me went far beyond his world-saving actions; it was the way he did what he did. I was captivated by his poise and panache. And I was more than just impressed. I was not satisfied to admire from the sidelines. I wanted to be like him. This is what heroes of the screen do to those watching them, and every great story has one.

God's story is no different. In fact, in God's story it is all about the hero. Preceding chapters look forward to him, the pages after his departure reel in the wake of his impact, there are very few subplots; everything points to the main character. The hero's name is Jesus.

Jesus' story has three important chapters. Chapter one is his birth and life. Chapter two is his death. Chapter three is his resurrection. Through them he shows us that he is God and that there is a new way to live, a new way to be human. God's story is an autobiography. It is all about him, but when he dramatically enters the script through Jesus it is as if the author sweeps on from backstage to play the leading role. These are to be the defining moments of the plot.

The events of his life also prove that the story has been about him so far. The older books about the Israelite people lay the foundations for his arrival, explain what he will do and predict in detail where he will be born, how he will die and many specifics in between. In total, our hero fulfils over 300 prophecies; the probability of him doing so has been calculated as as 1 in 10^{17} – a conservative estimate.[4] That's a very big number. Jesus knows where he fits in the story, saying of himself, 'The Scriptures point to me.'

His life itself is important. It can be easy when summarizing God's story to vault from Jesus' birth to death; to fast-forward from Christmas to Easter. In fact in the Nicene Creed, we do just this, hopping, skipping and jumping from 'born of the Virgin Mary' to 'suffered under Pontius Pilate'. Before we get to the cross and the tomb we must stand and admire the manger, hillside, boat and mountain.

Like a master artist, with the brushstrokes of his life Jesus paints a portrait of what God looks like: his compassion for the broken, his passion for people to be right with God, his wisdom to unearth the deepest truths of life, his power to defy the laws of nature, his grace to lift up those downtrodden by society and his forgiveness to restore others when he had been mistreated. His life alone marks him out as the most significant figure in human history. James Allan Francis wrote:

> All the armies that have ever marched, all the navies that were ever built, all the parliaments that ever sat and all the kings that have ever reigned, put together have not affected the life of man upon this earth as has that one solitary life.[5]

Aside from the billions who have identified as his followers, his impact on culture, political and legal systems, language, history, art and literature, not to mention when we take our holidays and the year in which we live, is monumental.

And yet he is best remembered for his death.

Christianity is synonymous with the cross. From church spires, jewellery and tattoos to national flags, the crucifix has universal iconic recognition. Many have observed how peculiar this is when you consider it is fundamentally an object of torture and execution. Like so many things, when Jesus touches something, a symbol of death and pain becomes an icon of hope and goodness. When he dies, Jesus takes upon himself the sin of the world, all the mess, our guilt, shame and brokenness. Past, present and future, they die with him. Our rebellion and brokenness that had previously been a barrier between us and God were destroyed in a cosmic moment of forgiveness. The consequences of turning away from God's story is death and permanent separation from him. But Jesus dies in our place.

But unlike many biographies, the story does not end with the death of the author. The demise of this hero is the beginning of the next exciting episode.

Early, on a dark and sorrowful morning, the hurting followers of Jesus, led by Mary, go to inspect his tomb. In grief and panic, they find the stone rolled away and discarded grave clothes. With explosive joy, Mary finds Jesus alive. Where they expect to find death, they meet life himself. The risen hero then makes several reappearances to hundreds of his followers, reassuring doubters, restoring broken relationships, sharing meals and commissioning the start of the church.

The Christian faith stands or falls at the resurrection. If Jesus is dead then Christianity is like most other world religions, whose founders are in the grave. At best he is a nice role model, whose teachings and example serve us well, but ultimately there is no deeper connection, no hope beyond the grave and you are probably better off centring your life on making money, trying to be popular and having some fun hobbies. But if he did rise again, that changes everything.

There are many atheists who have set out to disprove the resurrection because removing such a foundational piece is like removing an engine from a car, the processor chip from a computer, the steak from a mixed grill.[6] In many of these extraordinary attempts to discredit the story, not only do they find their task impossible, many end up renouncing atheism and choosing to follow the God they thought was dead. The evidence is compelling. It points to the truth that the grave is empty, the king is alive, that the story is not over and there is another chapter in both the hero's life and in ours. Christianity is true because the story is true and its author is alive.

Wally was a deliciously brown chocolate Labrador, with a wetter than usual nose and a boundless energy and enthusiasm for just about everything. Wally loved dog treats, chasing rabbits on country-side walks and shaking his wet coat after swimming in whatever mass of water he could find. But most of all Wally loved walkies. Regardless of the surroundings, pavement or pasture, Wally was happiest with his four legs in motion and the wind at his back. However, his owners' legs grew older quicker than his, time on walkies grew shorter and the more you looked into his sparkling brown eyes, the more you became aware of a yearning sadness. Then came the day Wally's owners took him on holiday. Beaches, pebbled paths, hills and fields lay before Wally like the summer holidays in front of a teenager. And he had the time of his life. If he wore a doggy step counter it would have run out of digits. Wally was so invigorated by his week in the countryside that as his owners packed up their caravan they had to tie him to a small handle at the back to prevent him running back to the beach or getting under their feet. And in a moment of terrible forgetfulness, Wally was left, tied by his lead to the caravan, as the car pulled away to begin the journey home. The Labrador's first thought was, 'More walkies!' However, as campsite track turned to country lane, walkies had turned to 'runnies' and 'runnies' to 'sprinties'. Even for Wally's energy levels, 'sprinties' could only last so long and by the time the caravan pulled on to a main road, 'sprinties' had turned to 'draggies' with Wally skidding across the tarmac like a four-legged canine waterskier. Wally was saved by motorists drastically gesticulating to his oblivious owners, waving frantically and shouting out of wound-down windows, 'You've got a dog on the back of your car!' Wally enjoyed most of his little adventure and had a few weeks' rest nursing chargrilled paws.

The moral of this story is that where you are going depends on who you are following. It matters that Jesus is alive. The celebration of the resurrection reflects the fact that our death sentence for sin has been removed. The Saviour knows his way out of the grave and his journey trailblazes the way for ours. We don't follow the memory of a dead religious figure. We can really know a God who is alive, who has pioneered a pathway to heaven and invites us to join him on the way. We can take comfort in a God who has experienced crushing rejection and brutal suffering, died and lived to tell the tale. This pivotal phase of the plot is the game-changer for our every day and our eternal destiny.

And there is more to come.

The church

I have wondered what it would be like to be the editor of a newspaper or the director of a news channel, to decide which items make the news and in what order. However, I feel for these people on so-called 'slow news days' when nothing happens that anyone wants to hear about and the news includes an extended weather-related feature and reports of a vegetable that looks like a cat (or for that matter a cat that looks like a vegetable). A friend of mine observed a newspaper in a small university town whose headline for that week was 'Local woman almost run over by car'. Most of the events in our world never make the news. Most stories are never told. A microscopic percentage is reported to the wider world, but even most of these are forgotten within twenty-four hours. Today's newspaper is tomorrow's chip paper, so they used to say.

But there are some things that happen that have a lasting impact, that the children of tomorrow will learn about in their history lessons, one-off events printed indelibly into time's textbook. And yet there are other events elevated into an even more elite category. These events start movements; movements that change the landscape of society. The life, death and resurrection of Jesus is an event of this magnitude. It ignited a global community with a whole new way of doing life together. It propelled people all over the world on quests to invite others to the movement. Life as we know it was never the same again.

The next chapter of God's story is about the beginnings of this international family, how they defied the odds of survival, a ragtag bunch of illiterate fishermen, dodgy tax collectors, women of dubious reputation and feuding brothers on the run from the authorities, while mourning the loss of their leader, who had just been executed. The church, currently 2 billion strong and growing, started from this unlikely rabble. Never bet against the story of God, or the God of the story.

In the books of the Bible that follow the stories of Jesus, this new movement continues against the odds, working out how to live in the mould of its founder, how to treat one another and crucially how to spread. Central to the latter is the dramatic turnaround of a bombastic Jewish scholar called Saul, a determined Christian exterminator, who has an encounter with Jesus and subsequently devotes his life to spreading God's story all over southern Europe. With the help of a few friends, he plants churches wherever he goes and then writes them letters. These letters form much of the New Testament, as the God-inspired wisdom teaches not just the churches of the time but resonates today as loud as ever.

The Bible finishes with a vision of the future, the promise that a new day is coming with no more hunger or thirst and the wiping of every tear from every eye. The resurrected Jesus will return and make all things new. There is an end to the story, so good it will satisfy every reader, with every cliffhanger settled, every mystery solved, all made well and happy ever after. But it is not yet, and until it comes God's story continues. He is doing what he always does, bringing light in darkness, hope in desperation, life to death and making old things new. In an ever-changing world full of heartache and challenges, the Author is still weaving storylines. He knows the end from the beginning and you have a part to play.

To delve more deeply into the themes of this chapter, for small-group discussion questions, more practical advice and video content, visit <www.storybearer.com>.

5

Telling God's story

Simplicity is the ultimate sophistication.
(Apple mantra)

Simplexity

Writing the last chapter was an immense honour and challenge. The story of God has captivated me from childhood and to summarize it as I did made me ponder, wonder and fall in love with it all over again. It also highlighted again its simplexity. Simplexity is a word my friend Len Sweet uses to describe the paradoxical combination of simplicity and complexity.[1] Allow yourself a moment of distraction at this stage. Cradle your phone in your palm for a moment.[2] From the home screen swipe left and right, allow the bright colours to captivate you again. That's enough ... put it away. You have just experienced simplexity. Behind those glistening pixels is a computer capable of connecting you to almost anybody on planet earth, pinpointing your exact location to the nearest metre, playing you an episode of *The Simpsons* and releasing all kinds of endorphins in your brain when you connect a row of same-coloured candies. And yet it is so easy to use. When my son Caleb was three, we had trouble persuading him to stay in bed until a reasonable hour. He would come into our room at a painful hour, the little hand on the clock pointing to four or five in the morning. Unable to tell the time, and upon receiving the news that it was not yet seven o'clock, one morning he astounded us with some manipulative yet creative behaviour. He reached for Dani's iPhone, hit the home button, keyed in her pin code (!), swiped across, opened the calculator app, typed

37

in the number seven and showed it to us declaring triumphantly, 'Look! It's seven o'clock, time to go downstairs!' Your phone is so simple, a 3-year-old can use it.

Like the phone in your pocket, God's story is both ludicrously complex and astonishingly simple.

The story of God is complex. Thousands of words, hundreds of mini stories, multiple types of literature all entwined into an overarching narrative. It is the greatest story ever told and the all-time bestseller. Scholars spend lifetimes plumbing its depths and my encouragement to you is to do the same. Throw yourself into the complexity of God's story. Like a dearest friend, devote yourselves to a lifelong journey of exploring the finest details, allowing the stories within the stories to embed themselves deep within you. Dig deep into the words of wisdom, seek to understand what was happening then and what it means for us now. Talk about the story, marvel at its complexity and intricate design, live the story out, and through it know its author better every day of your life.

But the story of God is not just complex, it is also simple.

Just as a 3-year-old can activate features of an iPhone, a child can understand God's story. When we begin to talk about it with others, it is unlikely they want the whole story all at once. Both for ourselves and others we need some ways of squashing and squeezing the overarching narrative into smaller, more compact vehicles of truth.

As a teenager, being given tools to do this was a game-changer for me in helping me share my faith. My parents sent me on a beach mission when I was sixteen, on what was my first experience of street evangelism. I nervously approached people, holding a clipboard with trembling, sweaty fingers to ask them if they would answer a few questions about faith and spirituality. I was surprised and encouraged to find most people were extremely open. The last question on the survey was, 'If there was a God, would you be interested in knowing him personally?' If they answered 'Yes', the deal was that you took them through a booklet that outlined God's story in four short statements that went something like this:

God loves you and created you to know him personally.

We have messed up and because of the wrong things we have done, we are separated from God.

Jesus died and rose again to forgive the wrong things we have done and enable us to be friends with God again, to know him personally.

If we want to accept God's forgiveness, we must choose to say sorry, trust God and decide to follow him.[3]

I remember sharing these four simple truths with a man on a park bench on that beach mission with great nervousness and teenage exuberance. At the end of the tract there was a prayer to pray if you wanted to trust in the God of the story and give your life to him. Having never done anything like this before, it came to the killer question: 'Is this prayer something you would like to pray today?' Astonishingly, the man said 'Yes'. He had never heard this story before, but he prayed a simple prayer and I believe something changed for him that day. I pray that it was the start of a wonderful adventure for him as a follower of Jesus.

Clearly there is more to the gospel than this; there are depths, facets and nuances that give God's story richness and texture, but if we are to be effective in explaining it to people on park benches, best friends and closest family members, we desperately need simple, uncluttered words to abridge the best story they could ever hear.

From left brain to right brain

As an evangelist, I am always thinking about new, creative and engaging ways to communicate God's story, especially to a generation who have never heard it. I was employed as an evangelist at twenty-two years old, having just graduated with a law degree. It was not the most natural progression, but I put my legal training to good use in the early days, collecting evidence from the Bible and my life and using it to formulate a compelling case why a young person should follow Jesus. The four short statements formed a linear, cohesive argument on which the evidence hung. But if you were to look at it on the Google-to-Gutenberg spectrum (see Chapter 3), it was a logical, left-brain and proposition-heavy journey. Over time, I observed the power of stories to engage and communicate God's story in a new way and used pictures, poetry and narrative far more. I haven't thrown the babies 'logic' and 'reason' out with the left-brain bathwater – helping people understand that it is rational to believe in Jesus is a vital step – but I've found communicating the gospel in a story connects with many people in today's culture in a way linear statements cannot.

Jesus was a master storyteller. From lost sheep to wise and foolish builders, from sowers, nets and persistent widows to good Samaritans, his stories attracted thousands of listeners on hillsides, and their legacy has stood the test of time. I would have loved to have seen him in action.

Prodigal: if I could only tell one story . . .

My favourite story told by Jesus crystallizes God's story into the finest and most spectacular of parables. Its narrative arc cut to the core of those of its first-century listeners. Men and women have identified with its characters for centuries, finding themselves wallowing in the pigsties, grumbling outside the parties and running down the roads of life. It has warmed hearts, invoked tears, reconciled relationships and changed lives (remember Ben in Chapter 1). There was a man who had two sons . . .

It is a really simple story. A son demands his inheritance, leaves his home, wastes the money, hits rock bottom, heads home and the dad welcomes him back. But like a pass the parcel at a rich kid's birthday party, there are some treats and treasures between the layers. If you have never read it before, open a Bible now or search online and find Luke 15:11–32.

First, let's look at the son's request to his dad, 'Father, give me my share of the estate.' To a contemporary audience, this does not seem too unreasonable, even shrewd if living in a nation with a heavy burden of inheritance taxation. But its first hearers would have been astounded, even offended by the notion: to ask for your share of the inheritance was to say, in essence, to your father, 'I wish you were dead.' The offence is heightened as this was a culture in which fathers were revered, respected and cherished. In doing so, the son would have severed all ties with his entire family and wider community.

Next, the son goes to a 'distant country', distancing himself geographically from his father, squanders the wealth in the suggestive 'wild living', morally separating himself from his father, and then gets a job feeding pigs. This is the final divorce, and to Jesus' listeners would have gone down like the proverbial pork chop in a synagogue. Because pigs were unclean animals, not just physically but spiritually, Jesus deliberately goes to extremes to portray just how far this son has fallen. In fact it would have been difficult for him to paint him in a more depraved light. He wants his audience to know that no-one can create a distance that is too far for a journey back to the Father.

Many of us have found ourselves in the pigsty of life and 'come to our senses'. The son writes a speech, leaves the pigs to fend for themselves and starts for home. The best he hopes for is a place in the household on the staff; sonship is off the table. There are many worse possibilities at this stage; it is highly unlikely that the extended community will accept him, let alone his dad. What he finds waiting for him is beyond his wildest dreams.

You get the impression that the father's eyes have never left the road down which he saw his son disappear. While he was a 'long way off', the dad sees his son and begins to run towards him. This action joins the long list of outrageous behaviours in this story, with Jesus' listeners at risk of developing 'shock fatigue'. For a man of the father's age to run would have been astoundingly undignified. He would have had to hitch up his robe, exposing his knees and looking ridiculous. The shame and embarrassment factor would equate to someone running down a high street in their underwear. Such is his desire and determination to reach his son – to welcome him, to forgive him, to protect him from the shaming and judgment of others, to love him, to reassure him he is home.

And to restore his identity.

Before the son can finish his well-rehearsed speech, his father interrupts with a speech of his own, commanding that his son be adorned with robe, ring and sandals. Take a moment to feel the explosion of emotion in the son in the embrace of his father. Memories of regrets and wasted years released in a cry of pain muffled by the dad's shoulder that is soon warm and damp with tears and snot. The adornments of ring, coat and sandals are all symbols of identity, authority and family. The dad's instinctive, instant response is to reinstate his son with the full rights of sonship. His failings are forgotten, his faults forgiven, his perversity pardoned, his abuses absolved. He is home in every sense.

For me, this is the best story in the whole of the Bible for compressing God's story into a bite-size chunk. We are all the child in the pigsty; God's eyes have never left the road down which we have departed. There is always a way back, a personalized robe with your name on it, a party waiting to be thrown and a multi-coloured, sparkling banner over the gates of heaven saying, 'Welcome home!' But we must come to our senses, prepare our inadequate speech and begin the journey back.

We all know what it is to be lost.

The frustrated kind of lost
when there's no-one to ask for aid,

where time begins to fade
and you wish you'd stayed . . .

At home.

There's the hopeless kind of lost,
where the money has been spurned,
where there's nowhere else to turn
and your soul yearns, your heart burns . . .

For home.

Because there's no place like home.

Home.
The place our hearts are based,
where our stories can be traced.
Where our bodies are embraced,
our memories interlaced with the smells
        and the tastes of home.

When the warmth hits our face;
entering familiar space
and our pulse drops its pace
and we breathe . . .

Because there's no place like home.

And yet we've never been, it seems,
in our ontological time machine,
so far from the scene
of our dwelling.

We're wayward, wilful, whimsical and wanton.
So far from Eden like we're an orangutan in Sweden.

In our culture we're like vultures;
consuming media like it's roadkill.

Forming sculptures with homepages
that will kill us 'til we realize . . .

There's no place like home.

And yet there's hope for home.
Because the desire isn't lacking,
like the prodigal who's packing
and the homing beacon's tracking us . . .

Home.

And the journey back's begun,
the central heating's on,
your room is being prepared,
the relationship's been repaired,
and grace is being spoken,
the door begins to open . . .

Because the cry of the apostles,
the deep incessant 'God pull',
the call of the gospel is . . .
'Come Home.'

And there's no place like home.

Come home

My son shares many attributes with me. Genetics are a terrifying thing. He is easily excitable, awake far too easily in the morning, is seriously competitive and always hungry. The two of us fight every day to get through to the next meal without some serial snacking. The struggle is real.

This impatience for food led a 3-year-old Caleb to approach the kitchen one morning and announce that he wanted a snack, or, being incapable of pronouncing one yet, a 'nack'. Dani, used to the request, calmly informs him that it is only 11.30 in the morning and lunch-time is not until 12.15. She should have remembered at this point the foolishness of negotiating with terrorists or toddlers. Caleb, in a state of 'hanger' (when hunger meets anger and makes you 'hangry'), spies one of my espresso mugs on the kitchen surface and reaches for it. With the white, porcelain mini mug in hand he turns, a newly found assertiveness bursting through his veins, raises his arms to their sides like a hooligan goading the police, puffs out his chest in defiance, looks at the mug and then locks eyes with Dani and says, 'No . . . Nack!' Dani keeps her counsel, shows extreme bravery by not being intimidated by the crockery-wielding maniac in front of her, takes a step forward and says, 'Caleb, I have told you it is not yet lunchtime. There is to be no snack and I hope you are not about to do what I think you are about to do.' Caleb, adrenaline coursing through his body, looks again at the cup, again at Dani, then back at the cup, before dashing it to the ground, almost certainly feeling like this is the killer blow of the argument, the sucker punch, victory is in sight. 'If breaking daddy's coffee cup doesn't lead to me getting a "nack", what have I got to do?!' He stands over the wreckage, with the pride of a lion over its prey, like a fighter over his defeated adversary, and in triumph declares, 'Mummy . . . NACK!'

Of course, it is fair to say that her response is not what he was expecting. Like his dad, he does not like being told off and is even less impressed with five minutes on the 'naughty spot'. I enter the action at this stage and wonder quite what has just taken place, with some of my beloved coffee gear in pieces all over the floor, a shell-shocked wife and a son screaming like a banshee. Dani tells me what has happened and I go to Caleb. His cheeks are hot and red, tears stream down his face and he is repeating over and over, 'I'm sorry, I'm sorry, I'm sorry.' Curiously, he won't look at me. His face is ashamedly turned to one side.

To me, the coffee cup is not a big deal. Like most of my hobbies, I have all the gear and no idea. What really mattered to me was the reconciliation with my boy. So I gently took his face and turned it towards mine. As the crying died down, I looked my precious son in the eyes and said, 'Caleb, I love you. I forgive you. It's going to be okay.' He then says to me, 'Daddy, I want to go home.'

The world is full of broken coffee cups. We only have to look as far as our hearts to see all is not well. But the offensive, comforting, outrageous, beautiful, scandalous and astonishing message of God's story is that he has the power to gently turn our face towards his, look into the depths of our souls and say, 'I love you. I forgive you. It's going to be okay.' All we have to do is come to our senses and decide to go home.

Telling God's story

We have explored the story of God from Genesis to Revelation and considered a few examples of how to summarize the narrative, but as story bearers we must also consider how we might communicate its beauty and depth with shortness and sharpness.

As I have travelled across the country and even across other nations around the world, speaking with people about evangelism, I have found that most people's understanding falls somewhere between simplicity and complexity. They have moved on from a simplistic understanding of the good news, but do not self-identify as full-time Bible scholars. Also, they have never given much thought to what they would say if someone asked them what Christianity was all about.

One of the most important things we can do is prepare ourselves to share God's story.

I want to urge you at this point to do some homework. If your best friend who is not yet a Christian asked you about what you believed, how would you tell the story? Your answer to that question really matters. Think about what you would say and actually prepare an answer. I don't know about you, but when I am in a conversation about faith, I often feel under pressure, and most of us, when we are under pressure, struggle to think straight. Being ready with a good answer to a good question makes a huge difference, will give you greater confidence and will also mean you are more likely to continue or even initiate conversations about what you believe.

I am not going to give you a set formula of how you might squash and squeeze the story of God into a short summary, but allow you to choose something that suits your personality and context. You may find that using the four simple truths work best for you, or the story of the prodigal, or a personal anecdote like 'Caleb and the broken coffee cup'. My encouragement to you is to have at least one way of answering the question, which may be to your friend the most important words they ever hear.

Yes, but how? Going deeper

- Take a pen and paper, or open a window with a flashing cursor on your electronic device. Write at the top: 'This is the core message of the Christian faith. This is God's story.'
- Take a moment to reflect, pray and think: what are the most significant landmarks on the journey through God's story? At the same time as thinking of these landmarks, think about the person in your life who you most want to know this story. Consider the following:
  - How does the journey start? How are we meant to live? I would use words like loved, purpose, meaning, belonging, in relationship. The story of our world and our relationship with God begins well.[4]
  - What is wrong in our world? On the journey of life, where do the bumps in the road begin to appear? I would use words like brokenness, lostness, selfishness, and explain that these are at the heart of the human problem.[5]

- – What is God's plan and his response? How does he make it right again? I would reflect on the big story of God, his pursuit of us through the narrative. It is imperative that you then mention Jesus and how he makes it possible for us to be in relationship with God again.[6]
- – What is the destination of the journey? What would a world look like in which we are back in relationship with God, both individually and as a world?[7]

- Then add some Bible references next to your landmarks. I have added in the endnotes of the above some that I would naturally be drawn to, but with the help of Google or a concordance you can find your own. When talking to a friend in natural conversation, you may not want to pull out chapter and verse as you tell God's story, but having a few key anchors in the Bible itself makes a big difference and increases your confidence.

- Once you have mapped it out, think about how you would communicate it to a friend who has just asked you, 'So what is Christianity all about for you? What do you believe? What kind of Christian are you?' Write it out in non-religious language.

- Practise saying it a few times to yourself. If you cannot do this on your own, you won't stand much chance when the pressure is on and someone you care about asks you to tell him! Once you are confident enough, grab a Christian friend whom you trust, tell her you are doing some homework from a book you are reading and ask her if you can share with her a shortened version of God's story.

- Well done. You are now a story bearer of the greatest story ever told.

More stories to tell

This is not the end of the book. When I was younger I thought that sharing my faith started and finished here. Preach the gospel and let them get on with it! But there are more stories to tell. Evangelism does not end with the telling of one story. God's story is not a closed book with the Is dotted and the Ts crossed, but an open play in which you are invited to play a part. The drama of history is still unfolding, and your storyline is intrinsically linked to the Author's.

To delve more deeply into the themes of this chapter, for small-group discussion questions, more practical advice and video content, visit <www.storybearer.com>.

6

Your story

Context is king

'I was about to give her a piece of my mind,' our friend told us as she sipped her coffee. She'd been sitting in the same coffee house a week earlier, preparing for an important business meeting. She was frantically trying to finish her presentation, but was struggling to block out her surroundings and concentrate. The cafe was full; a couple of business meetings, some mums catching up, an awkward first date, and on the adjacent table a mother demonstrating a complete lack of parental control over her two young sons. One of them was jumping up and down on his chair singing something about Paw Patrol; the other, slightly older, was flicking paper pellets across the tables at my friend's laptop. The mother was completely oblivious, staring into space. 'I had prepared my speech,' our friend recalled, 'and was clearing my throat to deliver a well-directed and well-meant complaint about the responsibilities of making sure children behave themselves when the mum just spoke first, "I'm terribly sorry, my husband has just walked out."' My friend shrank into her seat, offered some words of consolation and tried not to imagine what would have happened had she launched into her lecture on parenting.

Context changes everything. Context can completely change the explanation for a set of circumstances. Stories give truth context. They explain the why between the who and the what.

It is one thing to say to someone, 'God loves you.' It is quite another to tell your story of how unloved you once felt because of what you had done or what had been done to you and then to describe

50

that moment when you discovered that you were the object of someone's furious affection.

Your story grounds the intangibles of a relationship with God in reality.

Your story puts flesh and skin on the skeleton of what a life of faith looks like.

Your story gives context to what a life looks like when someone knows the God of the universe, when their trust is in a power greater than themselves, when they have recognized they are part of a bigger story and chosen to let the author determine their destiny.

In the Bible, Paul describes the change in his life:

> I have been crucified with Christ and I no longer live, but Christ lives in me. The life I now live in the body, I live by faith in the Son of God, who loved me and gave himself for me.[1]

But what does this mean? How does it make a difference? How does faith in Jesus actually affect someone's life apart from ticking a religious box on surveys and disrupting your weekend routine?

Your story takes your friend on a journey from the place of perceiving that faith is about a religious world view to the place of wondering how a real relationship with God might have a real impact on someone's life.

And you have a story.

You do have a story

As a teenager I would often go to Christian youth events. They were an opportunity to experience a big-crowd feel, meet teenagers from other churches and exchange MSN Messenger[2] details with suitors of the opposite sex from other groups. The Christian event of the 1990s had an effective, if not predictable, model of success. Two energetic hosts, usually extremely fashionably attired and wielding clipboards, would welcome a rowdy crowd, play a messy game and introduce the worship band. The band, after raising the bar on fashionable attire, would play two loud songs, in which they would try to get us jumping up and down, and then two slow songs to calm us down before the talk. Then the speaker would get up. The fashion bar at this point would typically be lowered (worship leaders tend to fare slightly better in this regard than speakers), and in many instances the speaker would, as part of his message, tell his story. It would usually go something like this:

> My life was a complete mess. I didn't pass my exams, fell out with my parents so they chucked me out. I slept on my girlfriend's sofa until she broke up with me and then I was on the streets. I turned to drink, drugs, kicking puppies and beating up old ladies to pass the time. I was a terrible person with a terrible past. And then one day I had just finished beating up an old lady with a drunk, drugged puppy and a blinding light hit my eyes. Jesus appeared to me and told me to leave my life of sin and follow him. I put the puppy down, bound the old lady's wounds, knelt on the ground and surrendered my life to the King. I'm now a youth worker, I share my story all around the world and even lead worship sometimes.

I hyperbolize and, for the record, am not in any way discrediting the stories told or the sincerity with which they were. The point I am making is that I would sit there as a 14-year-old and think that my story was comparably a little dull. I had stroked puppies, was fond of elderly women and the closest I had come to a drugs habit was my annual course of antihistamines, taken as hay fever prevention. As a result, while being inspired and amazed by the story, I was left thinking that I had no story to tell. Even as I got older and a tad wilder, my teenage years were less sex, drugs and rock and roll and more projects, hugs and sausage rolls.

The truth is that if you are a Christian, Jesus has changed your life. You have a story and it is meaningful, important, interesting and significant. It has the power to change somebody else's life.

Prepared

A close friend of Jesus, Peter, whose letters appear in the New Testament, gives some of the most important advice in sharing faith with unbelievers: 'Always be prepared to give an answer to everyone who asks you to give a reason for the hope that you have.'[3]

Always be prepared.

If I had one verse to hang the whole of the book on, it would be this one. I wholeheartedly believe that if we, as Christians, were prepared and intentional about sharing our faith in the everyday of our lives we might see something amazing happen and unprecedented numbers of people coming to know Jesus. We need to know God's story (as we explored in the previous chapters), but we also need to know our own story.

This verse is not telling you to have an answer to any possible question that your mate might have about Christianity. It is not demanding you have a sermon prepared on the book of Romans or the history of religion. Peter is asking you to be ready to tell *your* story. You need to have a reason for the hope that *you* have.

Are you ready? Are you prepared?

I was pretty tired. It had been a long day in London. I boarded the packed train, fought and apologized my way through my fellow jostling passengers to my seat and slowly began to tuck into the pre-packed chicken pasta I had bought for my dinner. The plan was to eat, put my headphones in, fall asleep and hope I woke up just as the train pulled into the West Midlands. The plan was set to be disturbed.

As the train pulled away, the train manager's welcome ringing in our ears, the carriage doors opened and, like an *X-Factor* judge bursting through the smoke, he made his entrance. 'Does anyone know where this train is going?' He was incredibly smartly dressed, wearing a dark, pinstripe suit over a bold red tie and his posh accent matched the high-powered look. Slightly less composed was his demeanour, firing questions at unsuspecting strangers while staggering from seat to seat, down the aisle, jostled by the movement of the train, almost certainly influenced by a few drinks. I was sitting halfway down the carriage, next to the aisle, at a table seat facing his ungainly waddle. Before he got to me his three or four attempts to strike a conversation were received with a very British smile and nod but no more acknowledgement, lest the discourse develop. To my dismay I realized that the aisle seat diagonally opposite me was available and the inevitable occurred. As he slumped into the seat he eyeballed me and asked where I was going. Aside from a few covered with headphones, every ear in the carriage could hear our conversation. The audience made me even more anxious. I told him I was going to Birmingham. Unfortunately, the interrogation did not stop there. Everything within me wanted it to cease.

'And what do you do?'

(Everything within me wished I did something normal.)

'I work for Youth for Christ.'

'Youth for who?!'

'Christ.'

'Oh, him!'

'Yes.'

This answer made my new friend curious, animated and slightly aggressive. To make matters worse, because of the quiet carriage, everybody aboard the 18.23 from London Euston to Birmingham New Street was now tuned in to the unexpected onboard entertainment of 'Grill Phil' as he quizzed me on multiple theological issues before turning our conversation to what happens when we die.

'What would happen to me if I walked off this train and someone barrelled me? Shot me in the face? Stone dead. Where would I go? Am I off to hell?'

I was completely on the back foot. I did my best to remember what people had taught me when sharing faith, but I felt like I was a boxer on the ropes for much of the conversation as each question came like jab after jab as I tried to hold my guard up. My mood was not improved by the guy across from me, whom I strongly suspected was a Christian (he was reading a well-known Christian book) and offered not a word of help.

It felt like the train had gone non-stop to Glasgow by the time he got up to go off. It was really painful. To continue the boxing analogy, as he prepared his belongings to leave his seat, I sensed the bell at the end of the final round and landed a minor offensive blow by giving him my business card and suggesting he keep in touch.

I came away from that encounter feeling thoroughly discouraged. I felt not only that I had done a bad job representing Jesus but, because of the public nature of the interaction, that I had missed a really good opportunity to share my faith with a whole carriage of people who might not ever interact with followers of Jesus. If I could go back and do it all again I would have asked him one key question: 'Can I tell you my story?'

This, in fighting terms, is the moment where you get on the front foot, on the offensive and prepare to land some significant blows. It should be every story bearer's signature move. In this case I was not ready to give an answer for the hope that I had. If I could replay the encounter it would be the single thing that I would change.

I learnt a second lesson that night: that God can take our feeble efforts and use them to have an impact. There will be times when you walk away from conversations with friends or strangers thinking you have completely blown it and done a terrible job, when you emerge from 'the ring' battered and bruised, with a fat lip and a sore head.

The next day I received an email – from him.

Phil
Thank you for your good-humoured banter yesterday evening.

Hope I wasn't too overbearing.
Best of luck with the good work – doubter that I may be,
I recognize good people when I see them.
Kind regards
Ben

Two thousand years ago, Jesus used a squashed packed lunch to feed a field of thousands. Today he is still taking our humble, small offerings and using them to make a difference. I will probably never meet Ben ever again. But if I did, I wouldn't be too surprised if he had decided to follow Jesus, and my fudged answers, poorly quoted Bible verses and defeated 'I don't know's, might have played a small role.

But this is no substitute for being the story bearers God intended us to be. In subsequent encounters I have fared far better because I was ready gently to ask to share the story of how God has changed my life.

You have a story, and if you are prepared to tell it, it can make the difference in connecting someone to Jesus. I want to take you on a journey on which we put together your story and you get to a place where you have full confidence, not just to answer the question 'Why are you a Christian?' but to even ask someone, 'Can I tell you my story?'

Yes, but how? Capturing your story

The first thing you need to do is to write it down. Take as long as you need, think about the key moments and, as you do, thank God for his goodness to you. Put as much as you can down on a side or two of A4 paper. Before you do, there are a few more things to bear in mind.

First, don't just talk about the moment you became a Christian. When we hear people giving their testimony, this is the most frequent part of the story we hear, and it is really important. But if someone asked me to talk about my relationship with my wife, I would do more than share the moment we first kissed. I would talk enthusiastically about the years since, describe some of our shared experiences and try to articulate how my life is different with her in it.

Second, you may find it helpful to answer some of the following questions:

When were the times you knew God was real?
What would your life be like without Jesus in it?
How does faith give you a way of understanding the world?
When have you known God to be close?

Third, one of the problems we face is finding the language to express what a relationship with the God of the universe looks like. I have found it useful to put together the list below, which are some of the changes the Bible says take place when we become a Christian. You may like to reflect on these words and choose some that are reflective of your experience and put them into your story:

Purpose	Family
Meaning	Wholeness
Forgiveness	Acceptance
Freedom	Identity
Love	

Once you have written it out, the next stage is to develop a condensed version. On some occasions of sharing faith, perhaps on long journeys or in late-night 'deep and meaningfuls', we have the chance to speak for a few minutes and, in these scenarios, we should give detail and can take our time. More often than not, however, we do not have this long. Especially in today's fast-paced life, our opportunity to tell our story might come over lunch at work, as we walk out of the pub with some new acquaintances, or in the terraces at a sporting event. Where time is short, the atmosphere is noisy and conversation lighter, it is better to have an abridged version, or even a couple of abridged versions so you can judge just how much to say.

So take what you have written and imagine yourself in a conversation on the bus with a friend who asks you the question for the first time, 'Why are you a Christian?' You know that they disembark at the next stop in a matter of minutes and that you have the time frame of the proverbial 'elevator pitch'. What do you say?

Practically it might be helpful to take what you have written on A4 and try to fit this shorter story on a piece of paper the size of a business card. The next stage is to learn and practise telling it. But before we get on to that, I have a question to ask you. Can I tell you my story?

My story

I grew up in the most beautiful Christian family, as the eldest of three kids, with a wonderful mum and dad. Faith was important in family life and I was dragged to church from the age of a foetus, right through my childhood. It was at a Christian festival as a 6-year-old that I remember first making a decision that this faith was going to be my own. In a big marquee, a few hundred hyperactive children were told that God loved them, that they needed forgiving for the wrong things they had done (I needed no convincing of this – I was a pretty naughty kid), that Jesus had died and rose again so that we could be friends with God and go to heaven when we died. I was even more excitable then than I am now, decided instantly that this was the best news ever and, when my parents came to pick me up, I eagerly told them I'd become a Christian. As a teenager, life was good. I had great friends and knew little hardship. The decision I had made as a child I consistently reassessed and made sure it was my own. As I navigated the teenage years, like many adolescents, I struggled with self-worth but found that a relationship with God and reading the Bible gave me a stronger sense of identity. I battled with my own self-doubts and pressures to conform, but knowing I was loved by the creator of the universe regardless of how I looked or what I did gave me a deeper sense of confidence and self-assurance.

The rubber really hit the road for me in one of the defining moments of my life when I was a student. I was studying for a law degree in Sheffield, and on a cold autumn day was having lunch when a friend of my mother's called and uttered some words I will never forget: 'Phil, this morning your dad died.' They hit me like a sledge-hammer to the stomach. Dad was amazing, a wonderful Christian, role model and friend. In that moment and the days that followed I knew I had a choice: to tell God to stuff himself for letting this happen or to trust him to comfort me in the pits of my darkest moments. I can honestly say, fifteen years on, that I have never known God so close as in those first few weeks after Dad died. The verse in the Bible that says 'The LORD is close to the brokenhearted'⁴ has proved itself true.

One of the best things about being a Christian is having a deep sense of meaning of who you are and what you are here for. I love it that we are more than just evolved flesh and bone, that we have a spirit, a soul, a purpose, and that we are loved by our creator who gives us good things to do and a cause to live for. I find my purpose in being a good-news person. After university, I joined a Christian youth work charity and spent my days sharing the good news of Jesus with young people and bringing hope to their lives.

In the latest chapter of my life's story, as well as knowing death and pain affect many people I love, I have been diagnosed with the same heart condition that killed my dad prematurely. I am well looked after by an amazing health team, but there have been episodes in recent months when I have woken in the middle of the night, my heart pounding and irrationally thought I was going to die.

I cannot tell you what a difference it makes knowing God is with me in those moments and that if the worst happened to me, my destiny is heaven. I do not know what my future holds but I know who holds my future.

Practice makes perfect

Apparently, one of the greatest pieces of rhetoric in human history was not planned. On 28 August 1963, Martin Luther King stood in front of over a quarter of a million people on the steps of the Lincoln Memorial. His speech writer had helped him craft what he was going to say and the paper before him contained no mention of what was about to become the most famous dream in the world. After he had been speaking for a while, the famous gospel singer Mahalia Jackson clearly thought he needed a bit of help and shouted from behind him, 'Tell them about the dream, Martin!' King, at this point, set aside his notes, fixed his gaze on the crowd and pressed the launch button on a defining historical moment, 'I have a dream . . .'[5]

If you have done any amount of public speaking, you will know that it takes an extraordinary amount of courage to leave your script, especially in such a situation. How was Martin Luther King able to deliver such a stunning address unprepared? The truth is that even if he was not prepared for this exact eventuality, he was more than ready for this moment as a result of the sheer amount of practice over the years. It is estimated that he gave over 2,500 talks and sermons in his life, racking up thousands of hours in anticipation of this moment. So when he grabs the lectern and launches into something seemingly improvised, Reverend King leans confidently on all that time he had given in intentional practice.

I am no Martin Luther King, but I do a bit of speaking here and there, and I have perfected the practice preach in the car on the way to the event. The windscreens in my cars over the years have heard Bible verse after story after joke after poem after prayer, and I have occasionally led them in a time of response to the message. Practice makes perfect.

When you tell your story, it may be the most important thing that the person listening hears. It is worth practising. Even a small amount of preparation will increase your confidence levels and the quality of what you say. It comes back to Peter's advice and charge to us to be prepared to give an answer to anyone who asks us to give a reason for the hope that we have. Practically, especially to start with, I find a quiet space, often waiting until I am on my own in the house, and rehearse telling the story that I have written down. With each run through you will grow in confidence and will be increasingly ready for when someone asks you about your relationship with Jesus. The next step might be to find someone you trust and ask them if you can share your story with them. This may then encourage them to think about learning theirs.

Knowing that you are prepared is a good feeling. Students with hours of revision under their belt, able to second-guess every possible question that could appear on the exam paper, walk into the hall with their shoulders back and chin up. Footballers who have taken hundreds of penalties on the training ground step up far more eagerly in a match than those who are irregular takers. Christians who know their story and are well rehearsed in talking about their journey feel calm and assured that if the conversation turns to faith they can get on the front foot. Know your story. Practise your story.

On to the front foot

Once you have the base level of confidence that knowing your story gives you, your storytelling can be reactive *and* proactive. You are ready not just to respond to someone who asks you why you go to church, believe in all that stuff or know so much about the Bible, but to take appropriate opportunities to say to a friend, 'Can I tell you my story?' This may be the question that leads to a moment of breakthrough, especially in a relationship in which conversation rarely dips below the surface into deeper topics. In these instances it is just as important to remember the subsequent line after Peter's charge always to be prepared, 'But do this with gentleness and respect.' As we tell our story, our tone must be gracious and without an air of superiority. We are not trying to compete and 'win' the conversation, but to invite the other person to come closer to God by understanding the impact he can have.

There are a few more things to be aware of as we think about story sharing. The first is that it almost always feels vulnerable. Even when you are well prepared, when you share personally and from the heart you can feel exposed, as if you are open to ridicule and attack. It can feel like that moment when someone steps into your home for the first time. But how it is perceived by the other person is different. It looks courageous. The etymology of the word courage is the Latin word *cor*, which means heart. This is also where we get the words coronary (relating to the arteries that supply the heart), core (the heart or inmost part of anything) and record (to learn by heart). In its early usage, courage was used to mean 'to speak with all one's heart'.[6] Courage is about letting someone into our heart and, when we do so, this amount of vulnerability can make us feel weak. But it is this raw courage that is seen by the person listening. That is why, when people open up publicly, we so often want to rise to our feet and give them a massive round of applause. Vulnerability is inspiring, brave and precious. Telling your story feels like weakness, but it looks like pure courage.

Second, against today's cultural backdrop, storytelling is popular. The increase in relativism, the idea that there is no absolute truth and that each point of view has its own truth, can be frustrating when talking to people about Jesus. If people hold this view it can mean they say things like, 'Well that might be true for you, but it's not for me.' However, there is an absolute truth and his name is Jesus. The positive side of this cultural trend is that people are used to hearing people's stories and are interested in them. Furthermore, via our live feeds on social media channels, we see our friends' stories every day.

Third, our culture is crying out for authenticity. At a time when the phrase 'fake news' is common vocabulary, when we see over 3,500 marketing messages on average every day and public trust in institutions, the media and religion is at an all-time low, we are desperate for what is genuine, true and real. Do not underestimate the power of your authentic story to cut through the counterfeit and speak truth to someone who previously thought religion was something you were born into, not a story or a person that changes lives. Your story of what God has done for you is real, credible and trustworthy. It has the power to make someone stop and rethink their life.

We all need to take Peter's command seriously. Imagine if every Christian was always prepared to give an answer to anyone who asked for a reason for the hope that they have. Imagine if we were all ready to tell our story and could share the basics of the Christian faith. I find that thought deeply inspiring. If all of us were significantly more confident and seriously better prepared, the effect would have infinitely more impact. Every person in the world would stand a better chance of coming to know Jesus. I want to urge you at the end of this chapter to listen to that great verse, think about your story and get ready. Be prepared, know your story – it might just save someone's life.

To delve more deeply into the themes of this chapter, for small-group discussion questions, more practical advice and video content, visit <www.storybearer.com>.

7

Living your story

Hypocrite warning

A few years ago, I was at a Christian festival. It was the afternoon and I was on a frequent mission in my life: I was in search of good coffee. My wanderings took me to the event's exhibition area. Now, if you are not familiar with the delights of such a territory, let me talk you round. There is usually a sizable Christian bookshop featuring the latest and greatest and Bibles of all colours, sizes, textures and shapes. There are the stands of some big organizations who have really gone to town with gantry and lighting displays to rival a Glastonbury stage, and smiling, T-shirt-wearing, iPad-toting volunteers ready to sign you up. There are some smaller stands of more niche organizations. What they lack in lighting fire power they make up for in freebies, luring in their punters with the a bowl of mint imperials, free pens or a prize draw. Then there are the Christian clothing stalls with some superb designs featuring delightful captions such as 'Faithbook, Jesus, Add as Friend', 'The J-Team, I love it when His plan comes together', 'Keep Psalm and Carry On' and, 'Ch__rch . . . What's Missing? UR!' Finally, possibly to prepare us for heaven itself, there are puppets. There are always puppets.

This exhibition was no different, and as the puppets stand was facing the coffee stall, I was honoured to be an unlikely audience member at their hourly performance where the stand owners showed what the puppets could do. Music began to play and two cheerful, colourful puppets popped up from behind a partition and energetically began to sing a remix of a well-known Christian worship song to a gathered crowd. Unfortunately, about a minute into the song the partition began to fall. Slowly at first, as a few pieces of gaffer tape gave way, but soon there was a gaping hole between the material and the top of the frame, and one of the puppeteers was fully visible with her hand up the back of an expensive smiling doll. Some people began to titter, some children's dreams were ruined for ever and surprisingly no effort was made to repair the damage. However, the most striking sight before our eyes was the severe contrast between the faces of puppet and puppeteer. As the song reached a rhapsodic climax, the puppet could not have been enjoying it more. For the puppeteer, however, it had clearly been a long week. She was so displeased with her current situation that she not only did nothing about the falling sheet in front of her but clearly wanted the world to know how little she was enjoying performing yet another rendition of 'Our God is a Great Big God' as 'Benji'. I am not sure anyone bought a puppet that day. Instead, what everyone left with was the memory of a euphoric puppet and their morose controller. It was this juxtaposition that made the whole scene so comical.

This is the problem that so many non-Christians have with the stories of followers of Jesus.

The word 'hypocrite' comes from the Greek, *hypokritēs*, meaning stage actor, and is commonly used when referring to people of religion who say one thing and do another. In short, the story coming out of their mouths does not match up with the story of their lives. The challenge for us as story bearers is that we tell two stories, one with our tongues and one with our actions. We need to do our absolute best to make them synchronize with each other.

Taste

The Bible has some really helpful images for this. On a mountainside two thousand years ago, Jesus said to his followers, 'You are the salt of the earth. But if the salt loses its saltiness, how can it be made salty again?'[1] In the ancient world, salt was a preservative; it was there to stop the good going bad. The way we live our lives is meant to bring out the God flavours of the world and tell the story of the victory of good over evil. But if we lose our saltiness, what story are we telling?

Shine

Jesus goes on: 'You are the light of the world. A town built on a hill cannot be hidden.' Light is a powerful image for the message of Christianity and what God does in our lives.

Light comforts. When I was a child I needed the landing light left on to let me know everything was okay.

Light guides. I love looking down from a plane at night on the approach to a destination and seeing the runway landing lights as we wheel around for touchdown.

Light attracts. I am always being told off in the summer for leaving the back door open at night as insects stream in, drawn to the warm glow of our home.

Light repels. For nocturnal creatures, light drives them back into darkness. I have also known this phenomenon when, being forcibly awakened by someone turning on the bedroom light, I have retreated grumpily back under the duvet. For some, the good news of Jesus pulls them closer; for others it pushes them away.

Light warns. Lighthouses stand as beacons warning of impending peril for ships near dangerous rocks.

Light exposes. When you bring something into the light, physically in the case of something you need to look at in detail, or metaphorically in the case of a difficult situation, it brings clarity, shows the thing for what it really is and means you can deal with it and move forward.

Light is beautiful. Whether it is pure light on shimmering water or fading, golden sunsets creating a warm glow. Light brings out the riches of colour in all its glory.

In their own way, each of these characteristics corresponds to a facet of the gospel. Light is a very deliberate image for both Jesus' own identity as light of the world and for us as the embodiment of that light as his followers.

Light is also visible. This is the characteristic that Jesus seems to be emphasizing in the passage by painting the picture of a city on a hill. During the Second World War, a blackout was enforced at night so enemy aircraft would find it harder to see where to drop their bombs. Heavy fines were issued to those who failed to cover their windows or who were caught smoking a cigar outside.

A city on a hill cannot be hidden.

A story bearer who lives her story out will comfort, guide, attract, repel, warn, expose, and beautifully stand out to those around her. Just by the way that story bearers live their lives, they cannot be hidden.

If we as Christians lived with our words and actions in sync with God's, as salty, light-filled people, the world around us would notice. Jesus goes on to say: 'Let your light shine before others, that they may see your good deeds and glorify your Father in heaven.' The impact of our actions is that those who see what we do will praise not just us but God. The way we live our lives draws others closer to him.

And the world is watching.

Sorry

Over the years, people have dismissed Jesus because of the way those who professed to follow him have behaved. There is sadly no shortage of godless activity done in God's name: appalling genocides and crusades, disgraceful abuses carried out by those in positions of religious responsibility and abhorrent treatment of thousands based on discrimination because of race or sexual orientation. We could go on. If this is the light from the city on the hill, it is not surprising that some have chosen to live in valleys a long way away.

Celebrate

We should rightly grieve, repent and apologize for our failings, while maintaining a sense of perspective. Especially when confronted with the soundbite that all religion does is make war, we should be proud that in the past, as well as the present, we have shone brightly as the city on the hill. Education and social concern have been part and parcel of the church's activities from the earliest days. Between 1850 and 1900, as many as three-quarters of all voluntary charities were set up and run by evangelical Christians.[2] From William Wilberforce, whose actions helped towards the abolition of the slave trade, to William Beveridge, who is credited with the reformation of British healthcare and the creation of the National Health Service, our story-bearing predecessors have let their light shine and we should be as proud of them as we are ashamed of those who have so badly got it wrong.

Moreover, the lights are still shining brightly. Modern-day Wilberforces look like Les Isaac, who began Street Pastors in 2003.[3] There are now 12,000 trained volunteers who strengthen community life and work for safer streets in over 300 UK towns and cities. Christians Against Poverty started in 1996 and since then has helped a staggering 63,641 households with debt relief, helping thousands of desperate people to become debt free.[4] It really is good news to the poor. The Trussell Trust was founded by Christians on biblical values and is responsible for a vast food-bank project, in 2017/18 alone handing out over 1.3 million food packages to people in crisis.[5]

As a church, we should unashamedly celebrate the impact we have on the world around us in bringing heaven to earth. From toddler groups to youth and children's work, homeless night shelters to care for the elderly, the social impact is immense. The Cinnamon

Network commissioned a study in 2015 to assess the impact that faith groups had on society, which found that local faith groups in Britain provide:

- 219,000 social action projects
- 125,000 paid staff
- 1.9 million volunteers
- 288 million volunteer hours
- support for 47 million beneficiaries
- support worth over £3 billion annually.[6]

We are good-news people with a good-news story. Let the light keep shining.

Read

After salt and light, the third biblical image is that of a letter. Paul, writing to a church in Corinth, says of the Christians there:

> You yourselves are our letter, written on our hearts, known and read by everyone. You show that you are a letter from Christ, the result of our ministry, written not with ink but with the Spirit of the living God, not on tablets of stone but on tablets of human hearts.[7]

The picture is that of God's story written on your heart, which is visible to be read by those around you. Leaders would say as I was growing up that my life might be the only Bible that some people might ever read. Our lives should be signposts to who God is, the truest and best possible way to be human, and should reveal, with clarity and intrigue, how amazing it is to be a follower of Jesus.

And I have found that the saltier you are, the brighter you shine and the bolder the type on your letter, the more people will invite you to share your story and tell with words the story you have been living with your life.

Conversation starter

My heart raced. My breath was short, partly because of the thick haze of smoke where we sat at the back of the top deck of the bus. School was done for the afternoon and it was the best bit of the day as my mates and I joked our way back home on public transport. My mate Adam sat on one side of me, Matt to the other. I was known to them as their token religious mate. When we would meet people I was used to being introduced as, 'This is our mate Phil. He's a Christian. But he's all right.' It was as if I had a debilitating illness, but at least you couldn't catch it off me. The subject of conversation was Matt. He had a problem, and it was one that no 15-year-old lad should have to face alone. He was going out with two attractive girls and was wondering which one he should sleep with first. Desperate times called for desperate measures. 'Phil, what do you think?' My expertise in this area was so limited, this was the equivalent of asking Scooby Doo about British foreign policy. 'Well . . .', I said as I cleared my throat, '. . . I think you should wait until you marry one of them.' After a few minutes of laughter had died down, the topic of conversation was about to change.

'No sex before you are married! Are you having a laugh? It's 1998, grandad!' This simple viewpoint led to a level of curiosity in faith that they had previously written off as inherited religion. The fact that I was willing to forgo something so precious to them gave me the opportunity for the first time to explain what knowing Jesus meant and tell the story of why my life was different as a result. I went home that night and had an awkward conversation with my parents, asking them to give me more reasons why marriage is so precious and the Bible tells us to wait until a wedding night to have sex. Armed with a few more reasons, I went back to Adam and Matt the next day. We did talk about sex – after all, we were hormone-filled, testosterone-pumped, laugh-a-minute teenage boys. But that initial statement that made them cry with laughter and ridicule was enough to begin a conversation that lasted the entirety of our teenage years, not just about sex but about all manner of matters of life and faith.

Living as a Christian in the twenty-first century means that many of your values are at odds with many of those of the world's. As you live them out, talk about them and are ready to give an answer to anyone who asks you to give a reason for them, conversations about faith will arise. You will have an opportunity to tell your story. But at all times we must do everything we can to avoid hypocrisy and ensure that our stories match up. A 2018 study of young adults asked what they look for in a leader.[8] Somewhat surprisingly the leading attributes were not vision, strategy, charisma, competence, hard work or inspiration. What the Millennial generation looks for in a leader is passion, humility and, most of all, integrity.

When we lose our saltiness . . .

The problem is that we are all human and even when we are forgiven, saved from our sin and in relationship with God, we face a battle every day to live a life worthy of our story. So what do we do when we blow it, when we do something that is completely out of sync with the life we are meant to be living and undermines all that we have been trying to show to our friends?

'Mate, I'm sorry. I messed up last night. Sorry for not being a better example of a Christian to you. Quality to see you. Until next time . . . Phil.' It was three years after the conversation about sex on the bus. I had just gone to visit Adam at university. We had gone out, partied too hard; I had drunk too much and I sat on the train on the way home with a sore head, disappointed in myself. Worse than that, I felt I had let both God and my mate down. The only thing I felt I could do was to apologize and try again.

71

Non-Christians do not demand that we are perfect, and we must not pretend that we are. There is a great deal of integrity in holding your hands up when you get it wrong and asking for forgiveness. King Solomon, an ancient Hebrew king, said, 'though the righteous fall seven times, they rise again'.[9] Many Christians fall short and then give up. When you get it wrong, pick yourself up, dust yourself down and go again. In some scenarios, it may well be that your friends are encouraged to see your human side and that you don't have to have it all together to follow Jesus (that's not a reason to sin deliberately, by the way!).

Live your story

Corporately, we have so much to celebrate, and may we never be shy about all that we offer to the world as Christians. But we also need to be bold and prepared for when, having opened our hearts, we have the opportunity to open our mouths. When you mess up, be real, say sorry and have another go. The world we live in is desperate for something authentic. Let's ensure that we present the message as the real deal, with actions that out-run and out-tell our words.

To delve more deeply into the themes of this chapter, for small-group discussion questions, more practical advice and video content, visit <www.storybearer.com>.

8

Stories to hear

Shut up and listen

Aged twenty-one, a young Italian by the name of Ernesto was determined to save the world.[1] So he began working for an Italian non-governmental organization who worked in Zambia and helped the local people with agricultural projects. The villagers seemed extremely reluctant to help out, which Ernesto and his colleagues wrote off as pure laziness. They found that the valley was extremely fertile, perfect for growing tomatoes. 'Thank God we are here,' they said, planting seeds and preparing for a bumper harvest. However, just as the tomatoes turned red, two hundred hippopotamuses emerged from the river and ate absolutely everything. The aid workers were distraught, frustrated and angry. The whole situation was a complete waste of resources. 'Why did you not tell us about the hippos?' they asked the local people. The response simply came, 'You never asked.'

Sometimes the best thing you can do is just shut up and listen.

So much of our training in evangelism stops after we have prepared people to communicate the gospel. However, the best evangelists aren't necessarily just expert speakers, but expert listeners. Sharing faith is not just about giving great answers, it's about asking great questions.

There is a third story (see page xxvii) intimately involved in the journey to faith, and it is the story of the individual person. Each person has a story, and without hearing it and understanding where that person is coming from, we may find our storytelling has very little impact. Donald Miller identifies the mistake thousands of businesses make in not hearing where others are coming from: 'Customers don't generally care about your story; they care about their own.'[2] Our friends are not customers of God and we are not salespeople, but the principle is the same: most people want to tell their story before they hear somebody else's.

Sometimes the best thing you can do is just shut up and listen.

The first thing we have to realize when we think about the other person's story is this: God is already at work in that person's life. Before we arrive on the scene, God is already at work. This idea comes from a principle in missiology (the study of mission) called *missio Dei*, 'the Mission of God'. This is the really important and encouraging idea that God himself is a missionary God who is active in the world. Reaching our friends with good news is not our idea that we invite God to join in with; God himself has taken the initiative, is already there and invites us to see what he is doing and participate in his mission.

Jesus talks about this ongoing movement of God to some Jewish leaders when questioned about his activity, saying, 'My Father is always at his work to this very day.'[3] Jesus' relationship with his father was critical to his effectiveness in his ministry. He models for us a closeness in relationship with his dad that is only possible because they are the same one God. But at the same time, this intimacy is the perfect example for us of how we are to live. More than that, it is the perfect example for us of how we do mission in partnership with God. Jesus goes on to say, 'the Son can do nothing by himself; he can do only what he sees his Father doing.'[4] It is quite an extraordinary statement for Jesus to make: even though he is God, he must rely on someone else to be fruitful. You get the impression that throughout Jesus' amazing ministry he spent each day in conversation with the Father, asking him what he was doing, offering his involvement, with eyes constantly looking for the signs of divine activity and a heart immediately ready to be opportunistic and obedient.

Sometimes the best thing you can do is shut up, look and listen.

I have a friend who became a Christian because God spoke to him when he was out shopping. I had a youth leader who started coming to church because he saw an angel outside the church beckoning him in. I can't explain why God chooses to intervene directly and proactively in the lives of some people and not others, but I do know that God is constantly working, drawing people to him, prodding, provoking and making known his presence in the world. Perhaps the starkest example of this came from an unexpected source as I read a business book by the Scottish entrepreneur and TV personality Duncan Bannatyne. Looking for some leadership and business wisdom, my heart picked up its pace and my eyes were on stalks as I read the following testimony:

> It was there and then that God said hello. I felt that I had been consumed by this presence, that something had completely shrouded and taken hold of me. It was unmistakable. I knew who had come and I also knew why. It wasn't a spiritual thing, it was a Christian thing . . .
>
> It was profound, and I stood there, stunned, considering the offer and thinking about what it would mean.[5]

I had read all about Duncan and had no idea he was a person of faith. I began to smile and inwardly rejoice; I love a good-news story of someone whose life has been transformed. Anticipating that the next paragraph of the story would tell of his conversion and acceptance of this God that had miraculously said hello, I was to be disappointed. The next lines read: 'I said, "No, I'm not ready" and God said, "Okay" and disappeared.' I genuinely started to cry. I was heartbroken that Duncan's response to the King of the universe making such a dramatic appearance was to walk away and say 'Thanks, but no thanks.' He had missed it. I prayed quickly in that moment, 'Lord please may I never miss it when you are speaking to me.' Don't miss it.

I then began to get a little angry with God. The story confused me, encouraged me, but I was also annoyed that not only had I never had an experience quite like that, but I had friends whom I had been praying for, for years, and they had never had something like that happen to them. Why couldn't God appear like that to them? If he did, unlike Duncan, I was sure they would follow him. I promptly apologized to God for being annoyed – who am I to question God's strategy and tactics? – and finally reflected that the story was a beautiful demonstration of *missio Dei*. God is always at work.

The question is: are we watching and listening to see what he is doing?

Life listening

Dale Carnegie wrote the famous book *How to Win Friends and Influence People* and said that the fundamental principle was that people want to feel important.[6] People feel important when they feel listened to and when others are interested in them. A friend once told me that interesting people aren't *interesting*, they are *interested*. Listening to someone, allowing him to talk about himself and being genuinely interested in what he is saying is a wonderful way of loving someone. At a time when we are encouraged to continually broadcast ourselves across several social media channels, and the busyness of life restricts our ability to find enough time to engage meaningfully with those closest to us, the world needs more great listeners.

How good a listener are you? Use the following questions to help you answer:

1 How often, when someone is talking to you, do you:
    (a) interrupt?
    (b) think about what you are doing later?

   (c) allow your eyes to glaze over?

   (d) update your social media status?

   (e) wish you had more interesting friends/colleagues?

   (f) nod off?

2 In conversation, do you ever find yourself just waiting for the next opportunity to speak?

3 If someone says something you don't quite understand, do you:

   (a) stop him immediately and ask him to explain it?

   (b) wait for him to finish what he is saying and ask for clarity?

   (c) not tell him you didn't understand – it probably wasn't important – you got the gist?

   (d) not tell him you didn't understand – you were thinking of something else anyway?

4 Where is your phone when you meet up with someone? Is it:

   (a) turned off and in your pocket? 'I am not going to be distracted.'

   (b) in your pocket but on vibrate? 'I should at least know how popular I am by the buzzing against my leg.'

   (c) on the table? 'I need to be aware of important notifications and ready to respond if something is urgent.'

   (d) on the table and ready for action? 'The person sitting opposite me is just one person in my world. There's a whole virtual network to interact with at the same time.'

5 When you sit down with a friend in a coffee shop, do you like to look outwards so you can people-watch as she talks?

6 Are your questions:

   (a) open? '*Tell me* about your day/what keeps you busy/about your hobbies.'

   (b) closed? 'Are you okay?'

   (c) imaginative and interested?

   (d) only asked because you want to give *your* answer to that question?

The word listen appears over 400 times in the Bible. It is such an important, underrated and under-celebrated skill. King Solomon says, 'let the wise listen and add to their learning'.[7] So how do we become better at listening?

Look them in the eye

A dating agency once undertook a daring experiment. They were convinced that the success of their matches would go up if they could get their couples to spend more time looking into each other's eyes. So they hatched a plan. Before couples met, they lied to each of them and told them that their date had an eye defect, but that they didn't want to talk about it. As a result, on the date, each person spent much longer looking intently into the other person's eyes, albeit for a phantom defect that didn't exist. But the headline was that the success of the dates went up significantly. Eye contact builds trust and creates a connection.

Ask more questions

'Knock knock.'

'Who's there?'

'Interrupting cow.'

'Interrup . . .'

'MOOOOOOOOOOOOO!'

That was my son's favourite joke when he was two years old. It would get us at least halfway up the motorway, and when it was wearing thin the cow could be substituted for a noisy animal of choice.

Interrupting is not a desirable listening attribute. It instantly communicates that what the other person is saying is not important and that you have something better to say. When responding to what people are saying, a good question is an excellent way to show that you are listening. If you have not understood something, wait until the person pauses before asking a clarificatory question. If you have understood, it is often good to summarize ('So what you're saying is . . .') and ask if you have understood correctly. Don't finish people's sentences. Don't immediately chip in with a better story. Ask another question.

Fight distraction

I am a people watcher. I love it. Above all other places I find coffee shops the most fascinating places to sit and wonder what is going on in the lives and conversations of other people. This means, if you were to meet me for coffee, on a bad day I would be tempted to look over your shoulder as you were speaking and observe the world around you. I have to continually fight the urge to let my mind wander and I have to choose to zero in on the person talking. To help me do this I will often choose the seat facing the wall to cut out distractions.

I also take inspiration from the Chinese symbol for listening. It beautifully summarizes the factors and features involved in good listening. Its five components come together in different elements to form the one complete symbol:

The ears – to hear.
The eyes – to see.
The mind – to think.
The heart – to feel.
Undivided attention – to focus.

Listening is a whole-body experience. I am particularly challenged by the last element on the list and determined that when I interact with someone I am not thinking about my to-do list, last night's football results or what I am having for dinner.

Show encouragement

I completely love the church I am a part of. I've belonged to the community there since we moved to Birmingham as a family when I was three. Now and again I have to say something at the front – lead a service, preach, give a notice and so on – and when I do, I know who to look out for. When you talk to some people, their expression does not change. Worse still, there can be those whose resting face looks distinctly uninterested or even hostile. But the best listeners, the people I look out for on a Sunday morning from behind the lectern, are those who listen with their whole face and respond with nods, smiles, raised eyebrows and the occasional emphatic 'hmmmm!' I seek these people out with my gaze because I appreciate the feedback. They tell me with their body language that what I am saying matters and that they are listening. This is exactly the same in conversation. Let your expression communicate your attention and be responsive to what is being said.

Listening and learning

What has any of this got to do with sharing your faith?

Evangelism is about connecting God's story and your story to the other person's story. You cannot do this if you do not know her story, and to know her story you have to listen. We listen, first, because we love people, and sometimes it's the most loving thing you can do.

For over a decade, my wife and I have been youth workers in our local community and have been involved in a number of projects. Some of these have been detached work, much like Street Pastors, where a team of volunteers will go out on to the streets, make sure young people are safe and seek to build relationships. One summer evening the team was just Dani and me, and we set out to walk the roads of our community, wondering who we would meet. We met Shaun. Shaun was fourteen, with floppy hair and a cheeky grin. He was also bored. 'What you doin'?' was his opening gambit. 'We're just walking around making sure people are safe. Wanna join us for a bit?', Dani offered. It turns out Shaun was also more than a little chatty. He joined us for more than a bit. He walked with us for nearly two hours and if you did a pie chart of air time, the Knoxes were a slim slice of the pie. We saw no-one else that evening, but we remember it as one of the most meaningful nights of youth ministry. We reflected that Shaun didn't seem to get the chance to talk much and what he needed from us was a good listening to. Not long after that, Shaun began to come to church regularly, and when he got baptized he asked us to be his Godparents.

Asking the right questions and listening to the answers allows you to build a picture of where this person is at with God. The more we understand the other person's story, the more we understand where God is at work in that person's life. Has the person had any experience of God before? Has he ever been to church? What have been the formative experiences in his life that have shaped him into the person he is today?

Joining the dots

The crucial next step is finding the connection points between a person's story and God's story. As you read the following accounts, think about your friends and ask yourself, from what you know about their stories already, what the connection points might be in their lives. Let me give you some examples starting close to home.

My wife Dani did not grow up in a Christian home; churchgoing was not part of her childhood experience. But God was on her case. A defining moment came in her life when she was fourteen and her parents split up, and particularly acute at this time was a breakdown in relationship with her dad. Out of this painful moment came a brilliant and beautiful series of events. Dani's mum, wondering how she was going to cope with three children on her own, was invited to church by her friend. Dani's sister had a Christian friend who invited her, at the same time, to the youth group at the same church. Dani's brother, who was at Cambridge University and has a brain the size of a small planet, decided to work out the meaning of life one night and concluded there must be a God, revealed in Jesus, and he gave his life to him. With all this happening at once, Dani didn't stand a chance. Swept along in the tsunami of family members meeting Jesus, she too became a Christian.

If you were Dani's friend, how might you connect the story of God to hers? One point of intersection might be the impact of the breakdown in relationship with her dad. Dani would say that growing up in those later teenage years without a father around made its mark. What would it look like, therefore, to talk about God to Dani in terms of the Father who is always there, will never walk out and will unconditionally love you and accept you? Interestingly, she says that the biggest question she grappled with as a teenage Christian was 'Who am I?' It was only when she read the Bible cover to cover and discovered who her heavenly dad was that she found her own identity as a beloved daughter.

For the next example let's continue the story of my friendship with Adam. I spent at least a couple of hours a day with Ads in my teenage years. We shared a bus journey, from where we lived to our school on the other side of the city, with two other mates, Matt and Jon. We were as thick as thieves and as silly as, well, schoolboys. Activities ranged from racing each other down the top deck of the bus with the seats as hurdles to conversations about love, life, homework and football. And occasionally faith. Adam had some unorthodox views about Christianity, epitomized by the idea that Jesus was an astronaut from another planet, his miracles a product of the advanced knowledge he had. This, he asserted, was the reason for church spires being rocket shaped, in preparation for us blasting off to meet Jesus in his own world. But he was (and still is) the most fun person to be around. Ads could turn the dullest biology lesson into a carnival. He was determined to live life for all it was worth and not miss out on a single second. As teenagers it made life exhilarating. It also got him into trouble.

His pursuit of pleasure led him, in his late teenage years, to excesses of alcohol and drugs; and even back then, I sensed in him the beginnings of regret for how he was living. I was far from an expert evangelist, but because I knew that feeling *alive* was so important to him, I would talk to Ads frequently about some words that Jesus spoke about life: 'I have come that they may have life, and have it to the full.'[8] His problem was that he saw the rules of Christianity in opposition to the free life he wanted to lead, so I tried to talk about real freedom instead; that we have so much stuff that actually enslaves us and only Jesus can set us free from it. For many years these conversations continued on buses, at the back of lessons and late into the night on the occasional sleepover.

When you demolish a wall with a wrecking ball, it often takes a lot of blows before the wall comes down. Some cracks may appear, but you don't see much of the effect of the initial impacts. Then, suddenly, the bricks will tumble. Our conversations about Jesus can be like this. We can say the same thing, in different ways, and tell different parts of our story, seemingly making no difference. And then in one moment, with one conversation, there can be a game-changing breakthrough. One August night I was sitting in the car with Ads and we were talking about guilt. He turned to me and asked me if I ever felt guilty for the stuff I had done in the past (having known me for the entirety of my adolescence, he knew how badly I had behaved at times!). I responded with complete certainty that I knew, because of who Jesus was and what he had done for me, that I was completely forgiven for everything I had ever done wrong. He would describe that moment as the one when the wrecking ball came through his defences.

Adam went home that night and, before going to sleep, he lay in bed and began to talk to God. He said sorry for everything he could think of that he had ever done wrong, from Class A drug use to cheating at Monopoly with his sister. He called me the next day to tell me that he had given his life totally to Jesus and that he had woken up, after not much sleep, feeling completely new. It was one of the best phone calls I have ever had.

I got so many things wrong in my witness to my mate. But, reflecting on the positives, I didn't give up, kept inviting him to stuff (despite lots of disappointing moments of rejection), and I was a good friend. I also think it was critical that I understood his story, what made him tick, and his preconceptions about God and faith. Without really knowing the theory, I was then able to connect his zest for life to the fact that that real life he was looking for can only be found in Jesus, and press into his feelings of guilt and assure him that he could be completely free by knowing God's forgiveness.

One more example.

I met Tom and Clare on the first night of an Alpha course at our church. Adam (thirteen years on from becoming a Christian) and I were leading the course. On a cold night in January, I sat down with Tom, Clare and the others in my small group over a spectacularly good chilli and rice, and we began to talk. I asked them what brought them to Alpha and what they hoped to get out of it. Their response was that they both had so many questions, but wanted to explore. They had been an item for a while and lived together not far from the church. As the weeks went on, we watched the videos, talked about their questions, and I loved getting to know them. They were brilliant at getting to know people and making connections. But as I heard their stories, one theme stood out more than any other: family. Clare was from a Christian family. One of the reasons she was at Alpha was that her parents had been encouraging her to go, and I got the sense they were longing for their prodigal to come home. Tom was from a large family with lots of siblings and sadly had lost contact with almost all of his relatives. When he talked about his past I could tell there was a lot of pain.

Drawing on the narrative of family, I decided to talk about my own story, of how the church had always been extended relatives to me and that in the hardest of times, being part of God's family had made a huge difference to my life. I explained that becoming a Christian involved joining the biggest family on earth, that a relationship with God meant being his son or daughter; 'to all who did receive him, to those who believed in his name, he gave the right to become children of God.'[9]

Towards the end of the course, Tom and Clare chose to follow Jesus. They also decided to get married as soon as possible. Seven months on from stepping into the church, they stood at the front of it and made their promises to each other before God. Beautifully, they also stood in front of some of their old family as well as some of their new one. Extraordinarily, around half the guests that day were people from the church, people they had not even met a year ago, and the best man that day was my mate Ads, the co-leader of the Alpha course.

Stop. Look. Listen. Live

Evangelism is so much easier when you hear the journeys of others, perceive what God is already doing and draw the storylines together.

So, may we know the story of God in its multifaceted complexity and its powerful simplicity. May we know our own story and always be prepared to tell it. And may we be as good at listening as we are at speaking, enjoy the voices of others as much as we enjoy our own, and find the strands that connect across the four stories we are exploring in this book. We will examine the relationship between the stories in the journey ahead, but before we do, there is one more story to tell.

To delve more deeply into the themes of this chapter, for small-group discussion questions, more practical advice and video content, visit <www.storybearer.com>.

9

Read the signs of the times

The way we do things around here

Culture is a weird and wonderful thing. At its core, culture is simply 'the way we do things around here'. Crucially for evangelism, it is not only individuals who have stories, whole groups of people do. And we must listen to that narrative as well.

When you travel to a different country, the longer you are there the more you become aware of 'the way they do things around there'. It isn't difficult to imagine the terrible messes that you could get yourself into if you are naive about the nuances of a particular place. While travelling in Europe I went to the toilet in a restaurant and began to use what looked like a urinal. I realized mid flow that it might have been a unisex sink. I'm still not sure. In Kyrgyzstan, Dani and I were given what looked like weak blackcurrant squash in a bowl and weren't sure whether to drink it, dip bread in it or wash our hands in it. While studying in France I was thanking some hosts for a delightful meal, and without stretching my linguistic abilities too far, said, 'Merci beaucoup', 'Thank you very much.' Sadly, I mispronounced the 'coup' and made it sound like 'cul' (still not sure what the difference is) and therefore apparently said, 'Merci beau cul', 'Thank you, nice bottom.' The moral of the story: don't be too effusive in your praise or you may end up praising someone's 'derrière' rather than their cooking.

Here are some other cultural customs to be aware of from around the world:

- Don't use red ink in South Korea. Red ink was traditionally used to write the names of dead people. If you write someone's name in red it could be misinterpreted as a death threat – slightly worse than saying they have a nice 'derrière'.
- Don't turn up on time in Venezuela. It is customary in the South American nation to arrive at least fifteen minutes later than the advertised time. To get there earlier is not just seen as keen but rude and self-indulgent.
- Mind your crockery in Germany. Before couples get married, at a little get-together, people start messing the place up. Plates, glasses and vases are smashed and the couple then have to clear up to practise doing housework together.

These are extreme examples, but they illustrate the way in which culture and customs can influence a place and the behaviour of people groups. Christians throughout the ages have responded to the culture around them in various ways. Some have decided that the one in which they have found themselves is evil or unholy and therefore to withdraw from it, disengaging from anything they perceived the culture to offer, that they might escape being tainted by its unholiness. At the other end of the spectrum has been a conformity to culture – 'If you can't beat them, join them' – and some have shown how easy it is to lose a Christian distinctiveness by becoming like the world around them at whatever cost.

Engaging biblically with culture

Jesus and Paul show us a different way.

Jesus was born into a complex cultural melting pot. His primary first-century influence was the Jewish world, steeped in ancient practices, traditions and narrative. But the nation of Israel was under the tight grip and governance of the Roman Empire, the Jewish people humbled and subordinated to their occupiers and trying to maintain a distinctive identity. The Jews responded to their Roman masters in different ways. There were some, Zealots, who were desperate for a revolution. They were ready to fight their way out of trouble. Herod and the chief priests were more pragmatic, sucking up to Caesar's power in order to maintain some delegated influence of their own. Others, like the Essenes, withdrew completely, heading off into the desert until it all blew over. The Pharisees believed if they just got themselves and the people holy then God would sort it out. Jesus neither withdrew nor conformed, but defiantly preached about a new kind of kingdom where neither Caesar nor religion was in charge, but God was king. He attended and engaged in the cultural festivals of his time, but used them to point to himself. He goes to the Feast of Tabernacles, a harvest celebration where the people thanked God for the water that had nourished their crops and prayed that it would fall again. At this celebration, Jesus says, 'Let anyone who is thirsty come to me and drink. Whoever believes in me, as Scripture has said, rivers of living water will flow from within them.'[1]

On another occasion, he is asked about paying tax to the Roman occupiers. He asks whose image is on the currency and says, 'Give back to Caesar what is Caesar's.'[2] For a liberating Messiah, this is not the counter-cultural, revolutionary talk the people were hoping for. But Jesus doesn't stop there; he couples the first command with a second, 'and to God what is God's'. And here is where it gets subversive – because the Pharisees and Herodians who asked the question knew their Hebrew Scriptures intimately, and that their opening pages decree that God made all humankind 'in our [God's] *image*'.[3] Jesus is saying that while your money might belong to the Romans, you belong to God. You are not occupied, controlled or owned by Caesar. Your allegiance is to a much higher power because you are fearfully and wonderfully made in the image of God. In one stroke he calls out the Herodians for becoming too friendly with foreign ownership and calls the Pharisees to a higher standard of obedience, one that goes beyond religious rules to complete surrender to God. His response to culture is to engage with it, use it to point to himself and be uncompromising in the decree that our loyalties lie above and beyond any culture, with our Creator himself.

Over to Paul.

Once an infamous Christian murderer, after a dramatic conversion experience, Paul now suddenly finds himself on the front line of Christian mission. Against a completely different cultural backdrop from Jesus, he trailblazes a path into Europe, speaking to Greeks, Macedonians and others who have no knowledge of the Hebrew story or the journey of a nation that led to the life and death of Jesus Christ. In this brave new world, he must navigate the culture in which he finds himself, while living and speaking the good news that has changed his life. Does he tear down the pagan gods and temples, capitulate and let their stream take him wherever it leads, or find a way to engage with his context and be as uncompromising as the Christ he is seeking to proclaim?

On one of his trips in southern Europe, Paul finds himself in Athens delivering a masterclass in cultural engagement. First of all, he goes to the marketplace. This was the forum of philosophical and intellectual exchange. Paul preached in the synagogues to the religious people, but he also went to the physical locations at the heart of where people talked about life, meaning and the universe. Second, when asked into the Areopagus, the epicentre of Athenian debate, Paul begins by finding common cultural ground: 'I see that in every way you are very religious.'[4] He then takes a prominent feature of the contemporary landscape and uses it to point to Jesus. He draws their attention to an altar he has seen in the city, which has an inscription on it that reads 'To an unknown God'. Paul majestically tells the Greeks that he knows this God that they don't, that this God is closer than they think and that Jesus is alive and has risen from the dead. As a result of this short engagement, some of those present trust in the God who Paul has made known to them.

What both Jesus and Paul demonstrate is that if we are to engage meaningfully with people we must engage meaningfully with culture. To paraphrase the theologian Karl Barth, preachers must hold the newspaper in one hand and the Bible in the other. In our modern world we might say that one should have our Bible app under one thumb and Twitter app under the other. Immersing ourselves in culture is not a new concept for evangelists and missionaries. The sixteenth-century Italian missionary Matteo Ricci achieved extraordinary success in East Asia, building unprecedented relationships with Chinese philosophers, scientists and emperors. Crucial to his success was his cultural awareness and adaptation. He was famously pictured in local dress, learned the language and used Eastern concepts to communicate the good news. Later missionaries, whether to Amazonian tribes, inner-city slums or middle-class suburbs, would spend years learning languages and customs before engaging in missional activity to ensure it was the most effective and relevant it could be.

We must do likewise. Most of us have mission fields that are on our doorstep or at our workplace rather than across land and sea, but that doesn't mean we should not be joining with Jesus, Paul and Matteo Ricci in asking what our world is like and therefore how best to tell the story. As a church, we need people like the sons of Issachar, who, we are told, 'understood the times'[5] and knew what to do. We also then need to listen to them and ask if how we are telling our story, with our words, lives and church practices, is engaging relevantly with our culture and helping those who need to hear the story hear it in a way that connects with theirs.

So with this in mind, what are some of the defining characteristics of our culture today and how might they have an impact on us as story bearers? Before we dive in, a couple of caveats. One: all generations have distinctive features. I will paint the picture of my generation, Millennials: those who came of age at the time of the Millennium, born between 1982 and 2000. Two: I will paint with broad brushstrokes. These characteristics will not apply to everyone, which is why we listen to the stories of individuals, but they will provide a canvas with the colours and tones of this generation.

Digital natives

The defining event in the lifetime of Millennials has been the onset of the digital revolution. Its impact has been far more pervasive than most of us realize. Far from just the technological advancements, the digital revolution has profoundly changed how we access information, how we think, how we communicate and how we relate to one another. It has changed our behaviours, our politics, how we spend our time and money and even the very wiring of our brains. In the course of human civilization there have only been a handful of progressions that we can legitimately call information revolutions. First came the development of speech and language. Then we began to write things down. Next was the progression of these hieroglyphic symbols and written text to the advent of the printing press: books, newspapers and mass communication. These media took us to the late twentieth century and the invention of technologies that would provide instant global connection, access to almost unlimited data, and the non-stop vibration in our pockets or palms of mobile devices enabling access and social interaction on the move. It is somewhat momentous that all of us have lived through some of this significant time in history. Millennials are known as digital natives, because they have grown up with complete familiarity with this world all around them. Most, certainly in their adult lives, have not known a time without wifi and mobile phones or a day without a cat video on a social media feed. Those in previous generations knew life before the digital world and, as those responsible for bringing the revolution to being, are known as digital pioneers or digital immigrants. I was born on the cusp of the Millennial generation, in 1983. I did my work experience, aged sixteen, at a large law firm that had one computer connected to the internet via the squeaks, beeps and squeals of dial-up. Less than five years later I had emails on my phone.

Welcome to the revolution. And hidden within the one big digital change are three distinct revolutions.

Three revolutions

The first is an information revolution. Imagine going back in time and having a conversation with your grandparents as young adults. The knowledge that they could access back then and the complexities involved in getting to it are in a completely different league from how we access that same information now. Imagine explaining to them that in the future, to explore facts on any given subject, there was no need to go to a museum or library; by holding a button on a gleaming pixelated 'lamp' and asking a question, a genie-like voice by the name of Alexa or Siri could tell you all you needed to know on almost any topic imaginable. Imagine their fright as you tell them to put away their local maps and begin pinching your portable screen to zoom into any location in the world and virtually walk the streets. The terrifying thing is that your time machine would not have to go that far. It was not that long ago that our nan and grandad were in their twenties. The last year in which we read more on a page than a screen was 1996. We now read sixty times more in pixels than in print.[6] The revolutionary pace of change has been so dizzying, we have at our thumb tips more information in seconds than those just two generations away could have accessed in our lifetime.

The second is a relational revolution. One thing that has not changed and never will is our God-made hardwiring for relationship. Being created for connection, we have sought to manufacture programmes, devices and websites that will satisfy this need, and the digital pioneers have not let us down. The digital revolution has introduced social technologies that have dramatically affected the way we begin, maintain and, as many angry, broken hearts will tell you, end relationships. Seventy-five per cent of Millennials have at least one social media account.[7] One in three of all US marriages start online.[8] We are able to conduct an orchestra of relationships without ever having to see anybody face to face. The reason so many of us are addicted to our devices is not just because they are our ticket to a library of hilarious videos, it is because they are the gateway to our relationships. The reason 53 per cent of Millennials would rather lose their sense of smell than their technology[9] is that they are created in the image of the relational God, and the relational revolution has put under their thumb tips the means to reach out and keep up to date with everyone in their network.

And there are reasons to 'like', 'share' and reach for the confetti emoji over the way social media has changed our relationships. Being connected to people no matter where they are in the world and the fact that we will never lose touch with our school mates is a good thing. Being able to share the ups and downs of life with people on social media is a brilliant thing; it becomes even better when you discover that life is hard for someone and that knowledge results in your meeting a real, tangible need, or when someone discovers you are a person of faith and it results in a real conversation in which you can share your story. For good-news people, social media is a gift and there is no better sight than a wall of happy birthday messages, the fast accumulation of thumbs up on a baby-scan photo or the news that the cancer is gone.

However, there are also reasons to treat our online activity with care. First, let us consider the quality of relationship the relational revolution has brought. A 2004 study found that the number of people in our lives with whom we 'discussed important matters' had fallen from 2.94 in 1984 to 2.08 in the year of the study.[10] What that piece seems to be saying is that we are losing close friends whom we trust and with whom we talk about the deep things of life. While our Facebook network might give us more breadth than ever before, there is a real danger that the depth of our friendships could be affected. While the quantity of our relationships has never been higher, it is possible that the quality of those connections is significantly suffering. Second, there has never been a platform created before that encourages comparison quite as much as the world of social media. Like the queen in 'Snow White', we daily raise our pixelated looking glass to our faces and whisper, 'Mirror, Mirror on apps installed, who's the fairest of them all?' From a glance at social media, it can seem that everyone else is having more fun, with more friends, in a faster car, on a more expensive holiday. And as we compare the worst of ourselves to the best of others, we compare our bloopers to everyone else's highlights reel. I have to fight this every day and I am so glad that I did not have Facebook as a teenager. Struggling with self-esteem already, I am sure looking at the polished profiles of my peers would only have exaggerated my insecurities.

The third revolution is an attention revolution. The internet is changing our brains. Our neural pathways are shaped by our behaviours, especially those that we repeat the most. If we are in the habit of constantly reading short snippets of information in quick bursts and spend less time reading long and detailed sections of prose, the wiring of our brain changes and adapts over time to reinforce these abilities and habits. If we talk more in text messaging rather than face-to-face conversation, we will become better at that form of communication than the other. Because the digital revolution is affecting our behaviour, it is rewiring our brains and especially those parts that relate to our attention. If our minds were battlefields, and our attention worth fighting for, the internet is a weapon built for mass distraction. Eighty per cent of teenagers check their phones at least once an hour. Seventy per cent of office emails are read within six seconds of arriving.[11] There is a whole world of amusement and excitement to be discovered one click at a time. We have never been more distracted or entertained. The digital revolution is affecting our capacity to concentrate on a task for long periods. The author Nicholas Carr observes, reflecting on how his

94

own attention span has changed, 'Once I was a scuba diver in a sea of words. Now I zip along the surface like a guy on a jet ski.'[12]

In tribute to the attention revolution I decided to rewrite Psalm 23 for a distracted generation:

My phone is my shepherd, I shall not disconnect
It makes me lie down in fields of distraction
It leads me beside noisy, colourful waterfalls of pixels
It clutters my soul
It guides me along paths of likes and shares
For my ego's sake
Even though I walk through the darkest valley of no wifi
I will fear no signal
For your 4G and offline features
They comfort me

You prepare a notification for me
In the presence of my followers
You anoint my thumbs with apps
My cloud storage overflows
Surely your updates and new features will follow me all the
    days of my life
And you will dwell in the palm of my hand for ever.

Weaving in the story of culture

So if the digital revolution is a prominent character in the story our culture is telling, how might we begin to connect it to the features of God's story and our story? Here are some questions to ask and some answers to consider:

- In the age of information overload, how do we help those around us cut through the noise to what is really important? An abundance of information does not necessarily equal wisdom. Jesus is the truest truth, the deepest meaning and the essence of what it really is to be alive. We need to distinguish a relationship with God from the rest of what life has to offer and communicate the uniqueness of knowing Jesus.

- Our hyper-connected world highlights our intrinsic hardwiring for connection. We can use this story to point to our greatest need of connection with our Creator.

- The online world gives us a space to be good news. Against a backdrop of young people saying that social media is the number one thing that makes them feel bad about themselves,[13] we need to embody and share the best news in the world on the newsfeed of our friends. While asking ourselves about how to do this relevantly and not put people off, we should not be afraid to use the marketplace of our day to tell our story.

- At a time when we have an abundance of connections, but their depth and quality is under threat, we should commit ourselves to costly, authentic relationships. Online friendship can be almost completely cost-free. Offer and acceptance comes with a simple click, there is no obligation to give any significant amount of time and superficial conversation can be maintained via the occasional reaction to a status via an emoji. Real friendship costs something. It demands our time, our emotional resources and, at times, our finances. It is inconvenient. As we model sacrificial friendship, we not only join in with God's story but reflect his nature to the world and our friends. And the more we lay down our lives for our friends, the more they will see the story of God at play in our lives.

- The life that we portray online must match how we live offline. As when we explored living our story earlier, where our words and works are out of sync, our friends will taste the inauthenticity. The digital world gives us another opportunity for hypocrisy. Do we wear an online mask or paint a true reflection of who we are?

- Responding to the attention revolution is a challenge. On one level it can create in all of us a quick-fix mentality where our desires are instantly gratified. If you want to listen to a song, hit 'Download now' in iTunes. If you want to watch a box set, get bingeing on Netflix. If you want a girlfriend, swipe right on Tinder. Faith and friendship journeys are not so quick, and so this narrative needs challenging. However, we must also be aware that when sharing our story, we are competing against a multitude of distractions seeking to capture the attention of our friends; being prepared, relevant and succinct where possible will help.

As story bearers, recognizing the digital thread at play in our world gives us an important insight into the cultural atmosphere. We are all increasingly sensing, perceiving and interpreting the world through screens, and this has a bearing on the content and style of the story we tell. It also gives unprecedented opportunities for the good news to reach people in ways that previous generations could never have imagined. However, it is not the only cultural marker of our time. Two more warrant exploration.

Anti-institution

Very early on a cold March Sunday morning, I drove into the centre of Birmingham and gave my name at a front desk to a security guard who looked even less impressed than I was to be up and working at the weekend. Pictures of celebrities and entertainers lined the walls as I was shown to a tiny padded room. To this day I am convinced the cleaning cupboards would have been more spacious. There was just enough room behind me to close the door as I sat at the desk, put the headphones on and stared at the imposing microphone in front of me and at a red flashing light. The headphones crackled into life and a voice said, 'Morning, Mr Knox, are you ready?'

I had been invited on to ten BBC Local Radio stations, one at a time, to respond to some research from the Vatican that had found that young people in Britain were among the least 'religious' in Europe.[14] I was asked why young people were no longer interested in faith and why the church was failing them. To each of the hosts' surprise, I said I agreed that young people were not interested in the institution of religion, but faith in Jesus was a very different thing. There was a degree of consternation when I told them that there was some even more credible research from Comres, six months earlier, that had found that just 18 per cent of 11–18-year-olds don't believe in God, and that 37 per cent of teenagers believe in the resurrection of Jesus Christ.[15] I don't know whether the listeners who heard me talk enthusiastically about the future of the church as they ate their breakfasts thought I was naive or deluded, but my prayer was that it might make them consider there might be more to the Christian faith than tradition and religion and feel prompted to find out more.

Nominalism is the idea that you would identify with being a Christian by name only, because you are born into a Christian country or because that's the box your family have always ticked. What is really clear from recent research is that nominalism is falling dramatically with each generation,[16] causing some to conclude that this is the end for belief in God and all forms of spirituality. But that is not the case at all, as articulated by my references on BBC radio. Across today's cultural landscape there is a rejection of institution, a deep distrust of those in authority and a lack of willingness to identify with tradition. Religion is out. But this doesn't mean that aggressive atheism is in. Far from it. Research keeps coming out that reveals a belief in something bigger than ourselves. A 2018 BBC survey found that while 62 per cent of British adults believe that some form of miracle is possible today, the percentage was even higher for young adults.[17] Nearly three-quarters of 18–24-year-olds said they believe in miracles – more than any other age group. As I talk to my friends who would firmly shun the 'religious' label, almost all would describe a world view where science cannot explain every-thing, that we are more than flesh and bone and that there is more to life than 'this'. While there are those who would have you believe that we are becoming increasingly secular, rational and anti-spiritual, there are some superb reasons to be encouraged that younger gener-ations are as interested in faith as ever.

So what?

So what does this feature of our culture mean for how we share our story? First, we should be encouraged that, while we have a very different story from our friends, we may share more in common than we might think. Do not assume that their default position is com-pletely atheistic and hostile to God. They may be like the Athenians that Paul encounters, have a belief in something and need you to point out who that someone is. Second, if religion is out, we should probably steer away from language that sounds like we are inviting people to join and sign up for another institution. If you are inviting your friend to church as if it were just another club or society, and frame your story in terms of religion changing your life, it may be less effective than telling your own story and talking about the dif-ference an encounter with God has made.

Individualism and community

The British sitcom *Gavin and Stacey* will always hold great signifi-cance for my wife Dani and me. As we sat on the maternity wards waiting for Dani to give birth to our son Caleb (she was in labour for *four days*), we managed to laugh and cry our way through all three series and the Christmas specials. One of my favourite scenes involves the characters ordering an Indian takeaway. Smithy, the larger-than-life best friend of Gavin, dictates his well-rehearsed order: 'Chicken bhuna, lamb bhuna, prawn bhuna, mushroom rice, bag of chips, keema naan and nine poppadums'. The suggestion is then made that his selection is put on the table with everyone else's and everyone can enjoy the curry smorgasbord of what each has chosen. Smithy's reaction is a hilarious rant in which he complains that his individual rights are violated by the suggestion, culminating in the declaration, 'In fact, forget it. I want no part of it. I'll order my own. I'll eat it in the car. I'm out.' Later in the episode we see Smithy, having calmed down, once again the heart and soul of the party.[18]

The clip beautifully illustrates a tension at the core of our culture that is especially stark for Millennials. On the one hand there is a powerful narrative of individualism. This is the iPod, iPhone, iPad, iTunes generation, where everything from coffees to TV packages, from flat-pack furniture to takeaway orders can be customized to your bespoke needs. We are the generation who were told from a young age that we can be whoever we want to be, and used social media to curate our own personal brand. On the other hand we deeply value friendship and community. We are more connected than ever before and aspire to be part of a network of diverse relationships that enriches our lives.

The mobile phone tells the same story. On the one hand it symbolizes connection, community and the web of relationships we crave contact with. To some degree it also displays a conformity; we all want the same technology, even the preferred brand of phone. On the other hand it sharply depicts the individualistic side of the coin. However, when the screen lights up, no two phones look alike. The wallpaper background is usually a photo, often a reflection of what is important to the phone's owner, most frequently a family member, boyfriend, girlfriend, sports team or occasionally, in a display of narcissism, the owner. The real customization is found in the choice and layout of the apps, depending on the user's preferences, tastes and habits. In the device that has become like an extension of our limbs, we find the perfect illustration of the paradoxical relationship that exists in Millennials between community and individualism.

Weaving this thread in

So what might we take from this thread of the cultural story and apply to how we connect with it? First, we need to take the good from the individualism narrative and challenge the bad. The good news is that God meets us where we are, he leaves the ninety-nine behind to come after the one; our faith is personal and God relates to us as individuals. We can celebrate and communicate the fact that, although there are 7.7 billion people on the earth today, you are unique, fearfully and wonderfully made. But we do not get to define ourselves. The challenge that we need to gently bring to our culture and articulate to our friends is that in following Jesus we choose to sacrifice our desire to have our life our own way and do it God's way. We do not lose our God-made individual characteristics but exchange an old broken identity and inherit a new one as a son or daughter of the King. To a world searching for an identity, we can share the great news that you can find out who you really are and become who you were created to be by knowing the author of your story. Second, we can go further and say that you can only really know who you are in relation to others. A new life with God is also about becoming part of the biggest community on the planet, full of all ages, backgrounds, ethnicities and stories. There is no more vibrant or diverse community than the church. That is why it is so important and why, when we talk about it, we are not selling a service or an association membership; we are inviting our friends to join the family.

Four stories told

This is the fourth and final story. While not as important as the first three (God's story, our story, the story of others), we need to be looking out for the signs of the times, as they make up the story-board on which the other three narratives sit. The church needs modern-day sons of Issachar who will predict the direction of cultural travel and help the rest of us stay ahead of the curve.

However, these stories do not exist in isolation. Like a delicately crafted feature film, while initially appearing to be storylines that run independently of each other, some interesting things happen when the threads are woven together.

10

Drawing the threads together

Interwoven

Crime thrillers make for frequent viewing in the Knox household (obviously once the children have gone to bed). Dani and I will regularly sit down and watch delicately crafted and casted TV detectives piece together clues, uncover the truth and retell the events that led to the victim's demise. Common to the plot in these shows are a couple of crimes that appear unconnected until author and director draw the connections, and multiple storylines are interwoven before being pulled tightly together like the individual strands of a rope. The mystery is solved, the murderer is found and the detective's hunch vindicated.

Something dramatic happens when connected stories are woven together. Like elements combining to generate a reaction, like ingredients mixing to make a recipe, or musical notes blended in symphonic harmony, the product of storylines being drawn together is often so much greater than the sum of its parts. Having described the power of the four stories involved in great evangelism (God's story, your story, the story of your friend and the story of culture), in this next section we will explore what happens when we blend their individual notes and flavours.

Family stories

I am living and breathing today because of a stick of rhubarb and a bowler hat. During the First World War, my great grandfather was fighting on the Western Front when he and his comrades came under gas attack. The effectiveness and potency of the gas was in attacking the windpipe and causing it to become blocked by the sides sticking together. Someone in the platoon knew this and, with some incredible quick thinking, also noticed that they were in a field of rhubarb. With extraordinary innovation and bravery, amid the panic, one soldier clutched at a stick of rhubarb with its celery-like curved stem and shoved it down his throat. Miraculously the plan worked, my great grandfather and the rest of the unit followed suit and were able to breathe through the cavity created by the fruit down the trachea. A piece of fruit destined for a crumble saved his life. After the war, another great grandfather was working as a foreman on a building project. While walking through the site, a sizeable piece of metal dropped from a great height. Health and safety regulations were not quite up to twenty-first-century standards, hard hat areas were not enforced and ordinarily this accident would have killed him. My ancestor, however, was wearing a bowler hat, which at the time was as functional as it was fashionable, and the fast falling missile simply bounced off his headgear. Those two men went on to father my grandparents and I am here today because of them and the supporting cast of fruit and hat.

Families have stories. The rhubarb and bowler hat episodes were relayed to me by my parents with great fondness and enthusiasm. Tales like these are really important in constructing a sense of family identity and even go beyond bonding families to building courage, spirit and character in children as they grow up. Research has found that the kids who are most able to handle stress are the ones who best know their family's history.[1] Furthermore, knowing these stories increases self-esteem and resilience. The same is true for our family story. The more rooted we are in God's story, the more intertwined our story with his, the stronger our faith will be and the greater confidence we will have to face anything life throws at us. The unknown author of the book of Hebrews writes: 'When you find yourselves flagging in your faith, go over that story again . . .

That will shoot adrenaline into your souls!'[2] To know the Author is what you were created for; being in relationship with him is your highest calling. Throw yourself into bringing your story closer to his.

Combining our story and God's story

Drawing our story closer to God's story does not just deepen our own friendship with Jesus and fulfil our purpose, it has a profound impact on the ability of others to meet him. Put simply, the closer we are to God, the more those around us will see him as they encounter us. Many of my friends smoked when I was a teenager and, on coming home, I had to allay fears in my parents that I was the smoker. Just by being in their presence I inherited their aroma. As we are increasingly rooted in the story of God and live it out, others will see what God is like simply by being around us and observing the way we live out our life, intertwined with that of the Author.

But to bind ourselves to God's story requires a deep commitment on our part to be continually nourished, influenced and captivated by the Bible story. Reading the Bible is not about academic study, it is not a religiously bound duty to a holy book, it is how we hear the Author's voice speaking to us today. It is how we allow the story of God to inspire us, instruct us and infect us with the contagious virus of holiness, truth, hope, love, joy and life itself. Getting into the habit of reading the Bible every day is an ongoing battle for almost every Christian, an often-quoted struggle that can make us feel guilty and inadequate. But winning this battle is so important. It really matters. Regularly grasping hold of the story and allowing it to grasp hold of you will have a significant impact on your own relationship with God and your effectiveness as a story bearer and good-news bringer to those around you. The effect of the television-watching habits of toddlers illustrates this perfectly.

How much screen time you allow your children is a common topic of debate among parents of little ones. In Caleb's toddler years, children's TV got us through the early mornings as one of us slumbered on the sofa, occasionally looking up to check the channel was cartoon related and hadn't switched to the Horror Channel. One of the phenomena we noticed through bleary eyes was the way in which classic stories and characters had been reimagined for a digital age. Prominent among them has been the computerization of Peter Rabbit and his friends, which had Caleb hooked as soon as the colourful pixels hit his eyes. From the moment he first saw the energetic theme song a few things happened. First, Peter Rabbit's adventures in Mr McGregor's garden became staple viewing in our household. Second, his bedroom became adorned with Peter Rabbit paraphernalia – toys, posters and books. Third, and most significantly, his behaviour became (and it's difficult to know how to put this) more rabbit-like. Having struggled previously to persuade him to eat certain fruit and vegetables, suddenly carrots were his favourite food. Playing imagination games with him involved Dani and I assuming the role of one of Peter's rabbit sidekicks as we raided Mr McGregor's make-believe radish patch. I realized the full extent of the fantasy when I was dropping Caleb off at nursery one day and instead of walking he got out of the car, adopted a crouch position, before hopping with both feet together towards the school gates.

What has this got to do with reading your Bible? Very simply, the more you read the story of God, the more you will become like those in the story. The biblical narrative gives you a pattern to live by, shoes to walk in and an example to follow. One of the primary goals of your life is to know the story so well that you become like the Author. The only way of doing this is to make a deep commitment, come rain or shine, when you feel like it and when you don't, to regularly pick up the story of God and ask the Spirit of God to speak to you through the story.

It is the verses inside you that will save you

I can testify to the impact and influence of the story of God in my own life. As I reflect on the times that I have been most alive, the most able to deal with disappointments and challenges and the days that I have lived the truest to the person I aspire to be, it is those days when I have spent time in the morning with my head in the Scriptures and my heart connecting to the Author. I have found myself at my best when the words of the story come quickly to mind. When I have been tempted to cross the street because I see a homeless person up ahead I remember the good Samaritan and my biblical mandate to 'act justly and to love mercy and to walk humbly'.[3] In the face of temptation, I remember Jesus in the desert, that my body is a temple and that I am made in the image of God. When I am discouraged, I remember how the story persistently insists that I am loved, that God is with me and that my suffering is producing perseverance in me, which is growing my character and making me hopeful.[4] And in the darkest of times it is the words that are most deeply engraved that will save us.

The Bible was central to family life as I grew up. As a child and teenager, I would crawl out of bed and stagger downstairs with bleary eyes and grumpy disposition, a condition exacerbated by the fact I had not yet discovered caffeine. Inked into my memory as I entered the kitchen is the familiar sight of at least one parent sitting in an easy chair reading their well-thumbed, dog-eared copy of the story of God. My dad would consistently ask if I had had a quiet time on that particular day. Reading notes were regularly refreshed and appeared at the beginning of each quarter on my bedside table. And all three of us children were encouraged to learn Bible verses.

As students, both my mum and my dad belonged to a Christian student group called the Navigators. One of the core habits that 'the Navs' reinforced was the continual memorizing of Bible verses. As a result, my parents were both not only very impressive in the number of verses they could instantly recall but were keen to train us kids in the same disciplines. So as I was driven across the city in my first few years of secondary school, before we could chat or put the radio on, we would recall our repertoire and learn a new verse. As a result, two things have happened. First, I have a pretty cool party trick. If you name any book of the Bible, I can instantly recite from memory a verse from that book. Second and far less superficially, I have in my mind a bucketful of nuggets of truth that have warmed my bones in the face of discouragement, rebuked and challenged me in the place of weakness and guided me home when lost in brokenness and doubt. And it was a memorized verse that once saved my family.

On the night of Saturday 30 October 2004, my mum sat in bed, her life having changed for ever in the previous twenty-four hours. Her husband had died, and the landscape of the road ahead was suddenly a road map of pain, grief and uncertainty. How would they survive financially? How could she raise three children on her own, two of them still teenagers? And where was God in all this? Instinctively she turns to the leather-bound book on her bedside table, perhaps more out of desperation than profound faith or hope. And she hears a voice drawing her towards a verse:

A father to the fatherless, a defender of widows,
    is God in his holy dwelling.[5]

I have no doubt that God can speak out of the silence at any moment to take us to a verse that will lift us and save us in any set of circumstances. But I also know my mum. Of all the people in my life, she is the one who knows the Bible the best, reinforced daily by those precious times reading and being consumed by the story. This verse that saved her could have come from nowhere, but my gut feeling is that God was able to bring it to her mind so quickly and powerfully because of her years of knowing and memorizing the story and love for the Bible.

At a similar time, while at university, I vividly remember going to bed one night feeling completely fed up, at one of the lowest points of my life. I was struggling to cope with pressures at home and at uni, and snarled and growled into my pillow in anger and frustration, desperate for sleep. As I woke the next morning, I felt as if I was emerging from a tomb. The words resounding in my head were words I had first chanted repeatedly in the car with my dad almost a decade previously:

> Because of the LORD's great love we are not consumed,
>   for his compassions never fail.
> They are new every morning;
>   great is your faithfulness.[6]

On that frosty morning, as I walked to lectures, my feet crunching on the icy ground beneath me, it was neither the fresh air nor a self-helping positive mentality that rescued me from a downward spiral. It was the God-breathed words of Lamentations, written 2,500 years ago, memorized in a Volvo as a 12-year-old, that brought warmth to my bones, hope to my spirit and a fresh perspective to my circumstances.

It is the verses that are inside you that will save you.

Launch pads and laybys

I am named, in part, after an early Jesus follower who is not only a brilliant evangelist but is also one of the few people to have ever 'teleported' from one place to another. The Bible introduces us to Philip in Acts 8 and zooms in to an encounter that he has with an official of the Ethiopian government. There are several lessons to be learnt from their meeting, but one of the key ones is the relationship my namesake has with the story of God. Philip clearly knows the Hebrew Scriptures intimately. His story and God's story are tightly intertwined and the first thing that this gives him is the confidence to engage in conversation with the Ethiopian. The better you know the Bible, the closer you are living the life God calls you to, and the more authentic the life you are leading, the more confidence you will brim with in conversations about faith. Philip's knowledge, first, means that when he sees the official reading from the Old Testament, he feels assured enough to say, 'Do you understand what you are reading?'[7] You do not ask that question unless you back yourself to explain it, are confident on the subject. This confidence opens the door for Philip to start a conversation about God.

Second, his relationship with the Scriptures enables him masterfully to navigate the conversation towards Jesus and the Ethiopian's need to connect with God for himself. It would have been so easy for Philip to show off his knowledge and for the discussion to remain philosophical or academic. Instead, we hear that 'Philip began with that very passage of Scripture and told him the good news about Jesus.'[8] The more you know the whole of the biblical narrative, the more you will see Jesus in the story and the greater your confidence will be in guiding conversations towards talking about Jesus. As a result of this interaction, the Ethiopian is baptized, and immediately afterwards comes Philip's teleportation moment where he is miraculously transported thirty kilometres down the road to a town called Azotus.

Weave your story around God's. Pull the strands tightly together. Take time every day to read the Bible, praying that its message will captivate your life. Memorize its precious words and let them draw you into a closer relationship with their Author. Put the story into practice as you live your life in sync with the life you were created for, its rhythm and values mapped out in God's story. The closer you are to Jesus, the more those around you will see him.

11

Weaving in the other stories

Christians should be the best friends in the world.

As Jesus was preparing for his death, in some of his closing words to his followers he spoke about friendship. These moments contain some outrageous words. At one point Jesus says to them, 'I have called you friends',[1] which was culturally ridiculous and contextually unprecedented, because his relationship with them was that of their rabbi, their teacher. And rabbis were not friends with their disciples.

This discourse also contains the famous words, 'Greater love has no one than this: to lay down one's life for one's friends',[2] frequently used when recognizing the heroics of those who have fought valiantly in wars, or sacrificed themselves for the love of others. These words carry immense significance too because of what happens next. Love is just words until action prevails, and with his arrest and crucifixion imminent, Jesus is about to prove just how much he means what he says.

Then there are these words: 'By this everyone will know that you are my disciples, if you love one another.'[3]

It's funny, because when we talk about the hallmarks of what makes someone stand out as a Christian, the way they treat fellow Christians is not usually up there. We favour other traits, such as church attendance, being well behaved or bearing a telltale cross round the neck or fish on the back of the car. But Jesus said our standout feature would be our love for one another. We should be the best friends in the world.

Let us flash back for a moment to Chapter 4 and the God who doesn't just desire relationship but is in relationship with himself. God is relational to the core. Connections and friendships were his ideas. When we become a Christian, the Spirit of this relational God comes and lives inside us and makes himself at home. With the founder of friendships, the king of community in our hearts, you would think we would be quite good mates.

Christians should be the best friends in the world.

And the world needs friendship. Because we are made in the image of this relational God, we are hard-wired to need connection with others. Isolation is deadly. Being without physical contact with others is as bad for your health as high blood pressure, high cholesterol, obesity and lack of physical exercise. It is more likely to kill you than smoking.

Most of us know the feeling of being alone. You can even be alone in a crowd of people. The feeling of not knowing anybody when you are surrounded by others who all seem to know each other can be emotionally agonizing. We yearn for a familiar face or for someone to break the ice with us.

It was my first full day at university. I had moved into some halls of residence and unpacked all my things. It is those kinds of moments when you feel lonely, waiting to begin the journey of friendship with someone. The pressure is ramped up in new situations like this one by people having said things like, 'You will make friends for life.' I sat there, having rearranged my stationery on my desk for the fifth time that day. Then there was a knock at the door. 'All right, mate? Fancy a game of pool and a couple of beers?' The tall bloke from across the hall was standing looming in the doorway. 'I'm Paul.' That introduction began one of the most important friendships of my life. Paul and I instantly connected and in 2014 I had the honour of being his best man as he and Anna got married. In a lonely world, friendship makes all the difference.

And friendship is not just what we were created for, it is also the best way to introduce someone to Jesus. The closer your life is lived to another, the more they will see your story. And if your story is intertwined with God's, your friends will see him and the difference he makes in every encounter they have with you. This is the very heart of what it means to be a story bearer. The thread of your story, woven around the story of your friends through friendship, and God's story through your connection with him, brings the relational strands together.

Friendship, however, is not easy. In a consumption culture, friendships often take more effort than we would expect. In an instant culture, trust takes longer to build than we are used to waiting. In a superficial world, deep friendship requires us to be vulnerable often beyond our comfort levels. But it is worth it, and here are a few ways I have found to be a great friend and build lasting connections with people.

- Be genuinely interested. As mentioned in Chapter 8 when we considered how we listen well, most of us want to talk about ourselves. Especially when we know we have an interesting story, have done something impressive or have great news to share, we can all be guilty of talking too much. Relationships are not built by impressing someone with how great we are, but inviting and allowing others to talk about themselves and their world is a completely different story.

- Be there 'when the proverbial hits the fan'. I will always remember calling Adam the day my dad died. His response was perfect. He was away for the weekend in Wales and on hearing my heartbreaking news, he leapt into the car and flew down the motorway. His willingness to drop everything just to be with me was all that I needed. All of us will experience significant pain in our lifetimes and the response of our friends in those times is so important. Often then the best thing you can do is just be with the person – make a cup of tea and sit together. The situation doesn't need words or extravagant gifts. Job, a man in the Bible whose name is synonymous with suffering, has some friends who aren't always very helpful or wise, but to begin with they do the right thing, sitting on the ground with him in silence for a week.[4] Do not underestimate the power of your presence.

- Talk lots. I am so good at communicating, I do so in my sleep. I discovered my sleep-talking habits on honeymoon when my wife would recall each morning the crazy things I had said in the night. It began on the second night when Dani, hearing a noise outside, tried to wake me, thinking something was wrong. I am an extremely deep sleeper and, despite shaking me vigorously, all she got in return was being told she was lovely and something about people boarding a ship. I think she began to have second thoughts about the man she had married, but has stuck with me thus far. And at the heart of our marriage, as in every kind of relationship, is communication. There is a formula that is central to friendship:

Time + Communication = Great relationship

- Journey together. As a family, we holiday in Scotland. Looking out across the vista of the eerie lochs in their stillness, seeing the misty glens in their peacefulness and standing at the foot of the mighty peaks in their majesty is good for the soul. The problem is it is a long way away. But we love the long journey. Why? Because there is nothing like being stuck next to someone for six hours to help you catch up on life. Journeys, whether physical changes in geography or metaphorical progressions through the stages of life, are the amniotic fluid in which friendships are cultivated and grow.

Some aid workers once arrived in Namibia and, observing the distance from the village they were working in to the nearest well, raised funds and built a pipeline between the two. Once complete, they moved on to help a neighbouring settlement. A few weeks later they returned to the original village to see how they were benefiting from having a water source in their village rather than several miles down the road. To their consternation, they found that all their handiwork had been undone. The pipes that connected the well to the village had been disassembled and lay in a tidy pile at the entrance to the village. Shocked and slightly offended, the workers asked the locals what had led to this display of vandalism. It turned out that the villagers preferred walking the route to the well. The journey, although long and arduous, facilitated conversation and relationship. It created strong social bonds between the women who journeyed together, not just the great physical distances to the well and back but also the distances of life.[5] Travel the roads of life together.

- Be real. Be vulnerable. We all have moments of brilliance. When something goes well for me, my reaction times to let someone know about it are lightning fast. I want my friends to think I am competent, good at stuff, and have been exaggerating my achievements for as long as I have had the words to do so. But we also carry fragments of brokenness. Bubbling away within me is an arrogant heart, jealous eyes, selfish desires and hurtful words that I fight to keep below the surface of outward behaviour. When they appear, I seek to cover them up and muffle their impact with the same lightning reactions of my self-promotion. With so many of my friends, I want their perception of me to be so dazzled by my brilliance that any hint of brokenness goes unnoticed. And yet I have found that when I let those close to me into the gallery of my imperfections, I receive in return greater acceptance rather than judgment and rejection. More often than not, this also leads to vulnerability on their part and a mutual discovery of common ground as they share similar struggles. Real friendship demands that we get beyond conversation that resembles Facebook statuses in its superficiality and takes us to a place where we can be ruthlessly ourselves before one another. There is something exhilarating, electric, even ecstatic that happens when we connect with someone in this deep, meaningful way. This

115

explosive energy exists because there are the same relational forces at work in the whole of creation. Open yourself up. Reach out and be vulnerable.

- Be honest. Occasionally I need a slap. Because of my tendencies to get too big for my boots, watch too much sport or say something inappropriate, I desperately need people to give me a metaphorical clip behind the ear and remind me who I am and whose I am. These conversations have happened frequently over the years (I am often in need of a telling off, which most often comes from my wife or my mum) but one instance springs to mind most vividly. A few days after we had been spending time with friends, Adam, who had been present, called me to help me reflect on the evening. I had no idea at the time, but in the group discussion that night I had been really rude, condescending and said some very unhelpful things. I was totally unaware of my bad behaviour. His phone call must have taken a degree of courage, but I am so thankful for it. Although a little bruised, I thanked him profusely and encouraged him to do it again whenever he saw me step out of line. Proverbs 27:6 says that wounds from a friend can be trusted. For these and the many other wounds inflicted for my benefit, I am so grateful. We need friends and we need to be friends who have the courage and care gently to reprimand and steer each other back on track. There are two further ideas here that need exploring:
  - Trust and tone are really important. Rebuking someone you have known for a week is a completely different ball game from someone you have journeyed with for thirty years. In many ways, you earn the right to speak into someone's life. Honest conversations of this kind can be really uncomfortable and you have to trust that you each want the best for one another. Think carefully about your tone. It is often helpful to be explicit about the fact this may hurt a little and that you want to address it because you love the person. You must be

gentle and tender without being overly apologetic. Someone once told me that when you speak into someone's life you take your shoes off. Where you are about to stand is holy ground.

– Evangelism is the purest form of honesty. You are telling the truth about the Truth. And sometimes, in a high-trust relationship, the best advice you can give is not what the other person wants to hear. In the sequence of events that brought Adam to the moment of becoming a Christian, catalytic was his girlfriend at the time breaking up with him. Shortly after this, he called me with a plan to get his life back together, which included a new flat, a new job and learning to drive. Needing affirmation and his self-esteem restoring, he asked me what I thought. As a natural encourager, I was ready to go, but I felt God nudge me to be honest: 'I think all that is okay, mate, but the only way you are really gonna sort your life out is if you give your life to Jesus and let him sort it out.' While he was less than impressed to begin with, I like to think my honesty helped him in the long term.

When you consider how important friendship is to us and how much work it takes at times, it is surprising how little we talk about it and think about the values and skills we need to build long-lasting, life-sustaining friendships. Let me encourage you not only to be a first-class friend but someone who seeks to bless and facilitate friendship wherever you can. To do so reflects the heart and activity of God in the world. As Jesus is strung up on the cross, he notices his mother and John standing near each other. With some of his final words, he says to his mother, 'Woman, here is your son', and to John, 'Here is your mother.'[6] Even in his dying breaths, Jesus is restoring relationships, creating families and bringing people together. It is what he does, and we should do the same.

We should be the best friends in the world.

To delve more deeply into the themes of this chapter, for small-group discussion questions, more practical advice and video content, visit <www.storybearer.com>.

12

Tightening the cords

'I've made someone a Christian'

My first job was leading evangelistic adventure weekends away. During the day, up to 250 young people from youth groups all over the country would rock-climb, abseil, zip-wire their way around an activity site, and later I would coordinate an interactive evening of games and entertainment before preaching the gospel and inviting young people to follow Jesus. I was a cross between Bear Grylls, Ant and Dec and Billy Graham. It was as exhausting as it sounds.

After my talk, there would be this amazing moment that fills me with gratitude and fondness each time I think of it, when those who had decided just then to become Christians stayed behind and prayed with their youth workers. It was to spiritual life what a hospital delivery suite is to childbirth. Every weekend we celebrated a host of newborn Jesus followers. Those who were already Christians or who had not responded left the large hall and hung around outside, waiting with some members of my team for the prayer to finish. One weekend, at this moment, an excited team volunteer called James bounded up to me, effervescent with joy and an expression of uncontainable delight on his face. 'Phil!', he blurted, 'I've just made someone a Christian!'

I didn't know where to begin. I guessed the sentiment. I assumed he meant that he had been chatting with a young person who, by leaving the hall, had decided not to become a Christian that night. I intimated that he had had a gentle conversation with the individual, perhaps shared his story or answered questions, and that as a result this young person had, after all, chosen to follow Jesus. However, the

119

phrase 'I've just made someone a Christian' has a hint of coercion or, at the very least, James taking a bit more credit than he should. In the moment, I could not help giving him a high five and celebrating with him, but we did have a light-hearted chat later.

Team game

The story does raise the interesting and important question about the roles and responsibilities of those in the evangelistic journey, though. In the example of that young person, who was responsible for her coming to faith? Was it James? Was it the youth worker who had been faithfully looking out for her for a couple of years? Was it their Christian mate who had invited her to the youth group in the first place and persuaded her to come to the weekend? Was it her aunt, the only Christian in her family who had been praying for her since she was born? Surely I deserve some credit having preached so well?! The thing is, when anyone becomes a Christian there will usually be a lot of people who have had an influence. It is a team game, not an individual pursuit. The other contribution of significant magnitude is God. Aside from the somewhat important part of making salvation possible by dying on the cross, there is also a major amount of divine activity in the journey to faith. We can all too easily reduce spiritual rebirth to human choice and instigation, and take undue responsibility and, at times, credit for what is a beautiful partnership between many of us and God himself. Paul recognizes this teamwork when reflecting on the growth in the Corinthian church: 'I planted the seed, Apollos watered it, but God has been making it grow.'[1] We all get to play a part.

The challenge with teamwork is that it is not good for two types of people: those who abdicate responsibility and control freaks. When cleaning a floor, the former disappear into the kitchen and are found with a half-eaten digestive in their hands; the latter won't let go of the mop. In a game of football, the former 'go missing in big games' and won't track back; the latter won't pass to their teammates and take every set piece. In evangelism, the former let everyone else get on with it and the latter do all the talking, take all the credit and don't pray for their friends. The final observation is critical. If we think it is all about us, we will not pray in the same way for our friends.

Prayer and evangelism

The truth is that God performs a central role in every life being transformed. When Lydia, a tremendously influential early follower of Jesus, hears God's story through Paul, the narrative tells us that 'the Lord opened her heart'.[2] Presumably without this spiritual cardiac surgery, it doesn't matter how good Paul's words were, they would not have had the same impact. An encounter with the God of the universe is not just a phenomenon of mind and body. There is such a dynamic spiritual connection that Paul goes further to say that no-one can even say 'Jesus is Lord' except by the Holy Spirit.[3] As a story bearer, you have an indispensable role to play in the lives of your friends, but it is not all down to you. The canvas itself and the finishing touches, as well as a few brushstrokes in between, belong to the artist of life. So how do we best collaborate with the master artist?

Like the threads described in this book, prayer and evangelism are intrinsically linked.

The answer is through prayer. Prayer puts everything that we are trying to do into the context of all that he is already doing. When we lose the desire for our friends to know God, prayer returns steel to our bones and fire to our bellies. For someone a seemingly impossible distance from becoming a Christian, prayer can unlock the door, break down the walls and bring the prodigal home. In the times when we run out of stories, when we do not have the answers to the questions being flung at us, prayer can save the day. And, perhaps most practical and helpful at this stage, prayer is the best possible starting point for helping our friends come to know Jesus.

I am astounded by how many extraordinary God-stories, real-life tales of people doing amazing things for Jesus, begin not with the words 'Once upon a time . . .' but 'So a few of us began to pray . . .'. When I hear of Christian Unions in schools experiencing rapid growth, the starting point was almost always a handful of teenagers beginning to pray for their school. I met a 12-year-old girl recently who had seen thirty-three of her school mates become Christians in two evenings in the park. This astonishing story began with her praying on her bed one night. When the Chilean miners trapped in the Copiapó mining accident in 2010 emerged after sixty-nine days underground, twenty-two out of the thirty-three had decided to follow Jesus. Jose Enriquez, a Christian preacher, was the only Jesus-follower when disaster struck. He was asked how he began to share his faith in such difficult circumstances. His response was not only to pray himself, but to teach the others to pray too. As he speaks of the experience he remembers the impact of his trapped colleagues beginning to talk to God: 'with fiery prayer the atmosphere began to change'. As they emerged from their rescue, they each wore T-shirts emblazoned with 'Thank you Lord'. Astonishing things happen when people start to pray.

You may be reading this book and already actively sharing your faith with everyone you know. But you may be reading this book because you not only have no idea where to begin when thinking about evangelism, but your closest friends, let alone your distant colleagues, do not even know you are a Christian. The thought of just admitting that to them seems completely terrifying. I hope you will get to that place. I hope you will go beyond that place to being able to share your story with them. I am praying for you as I write this, that through you they will come to know Jesus for themselves. But let us take one step at a time. And step one is prayer.

Stop and pray. Now

Stop reading for a moment and, before you continue, write down the names of five people you know who do not yet know Jesus. Pray for each of them now by name and, as you do, picture what it would be like for them if they knew how loved they are and some specific ways in which God might change their lives if he was in them. Keep the names somewhere safe and memorable to remind you to pray regularly for them. My challenge to you is to do so once a day.

There was a great American preacher called Dwight L. Moody. One day he began a list just like you. However, he was clearly (1) an optimist, (2) highly ambitious, (3) time rich and (4) very popular, because his list did not contain five names but one hundred. Wonderfully, ninety-six of his one hundred friends decided to follow Jesus during his lifetime! Isn't that amazing? What is even more amazing is that the final four were converted at his funeral! Imagine what would happen if we all had lists like Dwight L. Moody and were as committed as he was to praying for them. Imagine if in our prayers at church we prayed for lost individuals in our communities as much as we pray for the sick or disasters from the news headlines. Imagine what it would be like if your friends knew Jesus for themselves, and let that fuel your prayers for them.

My experience is that the more I pray for something the more I care. As I write this I have a family member who has cancer. The more I pray for him, the more emotional energy I expend for him, the greater I am invested, the closer I feel to him and the deeper my desire for him to get better. Put simply, the more the prayer, the more you care. This is completely true of my experience of praying for my friends to know Jesus. I have a really short list that I cover every day. Recently a couple on my list became Christians, but my list is so indelibly engraved on my mind that I have found it difficult to take them off. And as a result of praying for those on my list over and over again, I care more and more about them, that one day they will know the God who made them, loves them and is the only way for them to know real life now and for ever.

The long haul

But it is hard work and you have to be in it for the long haul. I don't understand prayer, but my experience of it is that things can happen either very quickly or very slowly.

Lauren was part of our youth group sixteen years ago. My wife Dani was the full-time youth worker at the church at the time and I was roped in to volunteer. Lauren was the life and soul of the youth group, had a fabulous sense of humour and was queen of the awkward question. When she turned eighteen we began not to see her so much and she stopped coming to church. Contact became sporadic.

Youth workers do not get enough credit for all they do in nurturing young people, and the impact can last a lifetime. As can the relationship. Lauren re-entered our lives a few years ago, where now, as a single mum, she was struggling to gain access to her young son. Who does she turn to for help in the moment of crisis? Her old youth worker. That is the power of the investment so many make in the lives of young people.

Dani was there for her in an extraordinary way and Lauren even moved in with us for a few months. But Dani also knew that, as well as the physical care we were able to provide, Lauren needed to reconnect with Jesus. We were just starting an Alpha course at church and it seemed like the natural thing to do to invite her along. However, on the morning of the first night, Lauren was having a terrible time and, using particularly colourful language, she informed Dani by text that she would not be coming that evening, that God was not answering her prayers and definitely wasn't real. So Dani began to pray.

Lauren's job was selling gas and electricity. She worked on a commission basis, knocking on people's doors and persuading them to change supplier. Having just sent this angry text, she knocked on another door and was invited in by a middle-aged man. Midway through the conversation about energy, she thought she began to hear God speaking to her. She felt that God wanted to use her to challenge and encourage her customer.

'Sorry, mate,' she asked, 'do you believe in God?' At this point you wonder whether he thought this was part of the sales pitch.

'I don't know,' he replied. 'Is this relevant?' What she said next was about to change his world.

'You've killed someone, haven't you?' she said from nowhere. The man's face went pale. Lauren's heart pounded. Where did that come from?

'Yes,' he replied. 'I've just served fourteen years in prison. How did you know?'

'Don't worry about that,' she said. 'God told me. And he wants you to know that he forgives you. And you need to forgive yourself.'

The customer sat there stunned.

'Shall we get back to your gas and electric bill? I think we can save you some money.'

I assume he signed up to whatever she suggested. Well, you probably would, wouldn't you?

When she left the house, Lauren called Dani to tell her the story. Having been not sure God was there, she was exhilarated by the whole experience, but then seemed to become annoyed with Dani, before asking her accusatorially, 'You've been praying for me, haven't you?'

Dani confessed she had.

Lauren bit back, 'Well I'm annoyed. Why would God do that to me? I'll see you at Alpha – 7:30.'

Lauren came to Alpha and a few weeks later Dani texted me with one of the best texts I received all that year: 'Lauren just called to let me know she has given her life to God.'

Sometimes prayer has an instant impact, like speaking to an energy saleswoman about forgiving a murderer to get her to come to church. Sometimes prayer takes a lifetime, like Dwight L. Moody and his four friends. I have been praying for some of my friends for over a decade with seemingly not much progress.

It is hard work and you have to be in it for the long haul.

I don't know how it works, but I do know that when we pray for people to meet Jesus, it draws the threads of their stories closer to God's. Somehow their storylines become increasingly interwoven with the reality of God in their lives.

But prayer has a deeper impact. It is not just about us getting what we want. It's about God getting what he wants in us; that is, him being more present in our lives. As we pray, we draw a person's story closer to God's but also our story closer to his. Tim Keller says, 'Prayer is not a way to get more things from God, but a way to get more of God himself.'[4] And I believe that the more we pray, the more willing we will be to engage in the lives of our friends, to live in a more distinctive way and to be the story bearers and storytellers we were created to be. If you are that person who finds yourself an undercover Christian among your mates, you may find that the more you pray the more you want your cover to be blown.

Yes, but how?

So how should we pray?

- We should pray for people to know Jesus. Paul, writing to his protégé Timothy, tells him to offer petitions for all people and in the same breath tells him that God wants all people to be saved and come to a knowledge of the truth.[5] Jesus, when teaching his disciples how to pray, instructed them to pray 'Your Kingdom come, your will be done'.[6] When we pray this we are asking that every corner of the cosmos come under the rule of God and this includes the individual hearts of our mates, as well as our neighbourhood and nation. In footballing terms, this is the ball hitting the back of the net.

- We should pray for opportunities to have conversations about faith, to listen to the stories of our friends and to tell ours and God's. Paul, writing to a church in Colossae, urges them to devote themselves to prayer, but also that God will 'open a door for our message'.[7] This is a dangerous prayer to pray. I have found myself praying this on mornings when I can foresee no significant interactions where a natural conversation about faith might occur, and by the end of the day a whole street of doors have swung open. In footballing terms, we create enough chances to score.

- We should pray for ourselves and others sharing faith, that we will have the words to say[8] and that we will make the most of every opportunity.[9] I find I can become easily discouraged at lack of progress or if I have blown or missed a chance to say something. We all need people praying for us, but we can pray too for our own encouragement and inspiration. In footballing terms, this is to pray that we stay match fit and keep landing our shots on target.

Here I am

The division of labour in evangelism is one of the great tensions we have to hold as we approach the Christian faith. There is no doubt that much depends on God, but we have great responsibility too, to pray continually for the kingdom to come and lives to be changed. We also have the great duty and joy of bearing our story, sharing the good news and being the best friends we can be. God never ceases being at work in the world, and he invites us into his mission, his great renovation plan for the universe. In the fields of eternity, we have our own vegetable patch to grow.

One of the best illustrations of this divine delegation I have seen takes place at a concert in Germany. Coldplay are playing in Munich and the clip I am about to describe is well worth finding on YouTube to appreciate its full majesty and drama.[10] Chris Martin is sitting at his piano and about to launch into another number in his vast repertoire when he spots a handwritten banner in the crowd, held aloft by an eager fan. Inscribed in black ink on a white piece of A2 card is an offer to play the song 'Everglow'. Astonishingly, Chris Martin addresses the wannabe and clarifies the proposal: 'Are you for real? Do you really want to come on stage and play with me? People have paid a lot of money.' At his beckoning, a young man begins to make his way through the crowd, is lifted over the barriers and takes off his hoodie and coat. The crowd are lapping it up, a sea of smartphones capturing the moment. Chris asks again, 'Are you sure you want to do this young man?'

As he takes to the stage with the confidence of a German penalty taker there is an amusing interlude where Coldplay's temporary band member takes his phone out, presumably to record the moment or take a selfie. Chris laughs and tells him he doesn't need to film it, 'Everybody's filming you.' Introduced as Ferdinand, the young German takes his seat at the stage piano as thousands hold their breath and wonder whether he can actually play or whether he is a musically illiterate fraud. As he opens with a pitch-perfect chord, they wonder no more and he is so good that Chris threatens to leave the stage and let the guy perform on his own. Returning, he says, 'Okay, let's try it, man . . . this is a German–British union . . . let's go.'

As he begins the song, two things happen that reveal cracks in Ferdinand's up-to-now assured persona. The first is that he fudges the first few notes, nervous energy presumably responsible for the errors. The second is that he starts too quickly, leading Chris gently to touch his arm and signal for him to slow down, before a reassuring, 'Beautiful, man'. The crowd show their appreciation for the moment before Chris starts to sing.

It won't be the first or last moment rock stars have harnessed crowd participation to crowd-pleasing effect. It is delightfully social media-worthy and will attract millions more online views than any other moments from the gig. But as I saw it for the first time there was a resonance of our relationship with God in mission. I believe that God could change the world on his own if he wanted to. I don't think he *needs* us. And he would probably do a better job – just as Chris Martin didn't need help playing the song that he wrote and would have been a far more accomplished performer of it. Yet if we are willing to stand up and be counted, to play a part in the transformation of the world, to put our banners in the air, God calls us out of the crowd and invites us to join in with his plan to renew the cosmos. And often that starts with the lives of our friends. Will you hold your sign up and invite him to use you in this way? Will you practise the song, know your story, pray for your friends? Will you join the countless ordinary men and women who have said to God through the ages, 'Here I am, send me'?

There are a few more things I love about the clip. First, I love how, when he is out of time and out of key at the beginning, Chris Martin slows his accompanist down, guides him and steers him back on track. As we embark on the adventure of sharing our faith, we will inevitably make mistakes. I have blown opportunities, bottled conversations, been over the top, exaggerated the truth, underplayed the truth, fluffed my lines and not known what to say. My experience is that God uses every single one of these faux pas to shape, hone and grow me, not only as an evangelist but in my own character as well. But if you don't have a go in the first place you will never have the growth opportunity.

Second, there is a tender episode during the song when Chris sings the line, 'This particular diamond was extra special'. As he sings it, he places his hand on Ferdinand's shoulder and gives it a father-like squeeze, linking the line to the young performer as if to tell him how proud he is of him and how glad of this moment. It is incredibly important to know that God will not love you any more if you lead every single one of your friends to Jesus. And he will not love you any less if you never have a conversation about him. But my experience has been that, as I have stepped out, most often to uncomfortable levels where I have had to depend more on him, I have felt him with me in an especially close way, his hand on my shoulder and his smile at my back.

Third, there is that wonderful moment where Ferdinand is told to put his phone away, which epitomizes a generational attitude to want to capture each frame of life and share it with the world. Chris's pointing out that everyone is filming reminds us that the world is watching and even more so when we decide to step out and tell our story. Even letting others know that you are a Christian will bring a world of preconceptions to their mind. For some, you will be the only Christian they have ever met. Some will have an experience of church and a frame of reference in which to place you. For others, you will be to them like a member of a faraway tribe or a relic from history; they were aware that people like you existed, but they may never have expected to meet one of you. It can be both exhilarating and refreshing to break down preconceived stereotypes, while at the same time a challenge, as many may instantly judge you and associate you with a world view that is, to them, outdated and even harmful. When we hold our sign aloft and invite God to call us out of the crowd, we risk prejudice and disapproval, we have the opportunity to change mindsets and, most importantly, we climb on to the stage to play our part in the collaborative mission of God in the world.

If you are stuck not knowing where to begin with bearing and sharing your story, not knowing whether you have the confidence to raise your sign from among the crowd, just start praying. That, in itself, demonstrates to God your heart for your friends. It indicates your availability to him. It draws the threads of their story and God's that little bit closer together. It warms your heart and motivates you to love them more deeply. It is that love you have for them and the love you have for Jesus that will stir you to tell your story to them.

Great tales of lives changed begin not with 'Once upon a time . . .' but with 'So we started to pray . . .'.

To delve more deeply into the themes of this chapter, for small-group discussion questions, more practical advice and video content, visit <www.storybearer.com>.

13

What must I do to be saved?

All that we have discussed so far points in a certain direction. Becoming familiar with our story and God's story, striving to listen well and be the best friend we can be and praying our hearts out for our friends should steer us towards a destination: lives being changed. We have recalled our moments when we decided to follow Jesus, and spoken much about how to help people on their own journey towards God. But what do we do when they get there? This chapter will prevent panic, keep your heart rate in check and give you the confidence you need when the moment comes and someone says to you, 'I'm ready . . .'.

Goals and glory

I have played for a number of different football teams over the years and with players of wildly different abilities. I love the dynamic of teams of all kinds and enjoy finding my place, assuming different roles to suit the situation and adapting to those around me. I once played for a football team that was full of exceptionally talented individuals, in which I was one of the weaker members. Each player in the team was superb on the ball, assured in possession and extremely accurate when passing the ball. We were so good in fact that we hardly ever gave the ball away and the other team barely got a touch. We worked well as a team, each understanding what the others wanted from us and moving well about the pitch. However, despite our dominance, our results did not reflect our abilities. Our team lacked a crucial piece: we had no-one in the team who could put the ball in the back of the net.

As a lover of stories, I love the climactic ending of a compelling book or film. In a good story, you don't need the decreasing pages under your right thumb to sense it coming. The author moves the key players into position, raises the tension levels and leaves enough doubt in your mind that all may not end well. You feel acutely the potential impact of triumph and disaster and root for the hero as if that person was your closest relation.

You crave resolution.

And then it arrives.

When it does, you descend the crest of relief and the author leaves you with a sense that all is now well. The battle is fought, love has been found, evil has been defeated, the quest completed, a relationship restored, the killer unmasked, the guilty punished, the innocent freed, the world is saved and our hero can ride off into the sunset.

But have you ever known what it feels like to come to the end of a story feeling dissatisfied? Sometimes this happens because the outcome is not what we would have wanted. Sometimes because the happy ending is a little too sickly sweet. Sometimes because it was all a bit too easy or obvious. But the worst type of ending is no ending at all. You reach 'THE END' with a headful of questions. Too many threads of storylines are left untangled and untied. You have spent hours and hours building up to a resolution that is never reached in one way or another.

We need to know how to put the ball in the back of the net.

We need to know how to finish the story.

How to help someone make the most important decision of his or her life

A few years had passed since the moment I had suggested to Adam and Matt on the top deck of a bus that they wait until they were married to have sex (see Chapter 7). Adam was yet to have his moment of decision (see Chapter 8). Matt and I had been having some significant conversations about God and we were away on a Christian waterskiing holiday. One afternoon by the lake, a huge sheet of tarpaulin came out, got covered in washing-up liquid and water, and we were all throwing ourselves down it at breakneck speed. In a moment of madness, a friend and I suggested we start at opposite ends of the slide and go 'head to head'. And that is how it ended up. I think we realized it was a stupid idea when we began our run-ups, but by that stage it was too late, male pride and peer pressure would dictate that we would not back out now and as our heads hurtled towards one another the inevitable occurred. The first thing I remember was not being able to see out of my left eye. It turned out that was because my eyebrow had borne the brunt of the impact and was now dangling over the eye. A lot of blood mixed with the washing-up liquid.

Matt came with me to hospital and as I sat with a bandage around my head, awaiting a permanent stitched solution, we continued to chat about God. At first, I thought I might be imagining it, the concussion causing me to hallucinate. As we sat in the hospital waiting room, Matt, after years of prayer and trying to share my faith with him, turned to me and said, 'I'm ready to become a Christian. What do I do?'

I sat there, scarcely believing what I was hearing.

The elation dissipated any throbbing still going on in my head. I was so happy, but I suddenly became aware that I was not totally sure how to answer his question. No-one had ever told me what to do in this situation.

As I have spoken to hundreds of Christians about this moment, I have become extremely concerned at how ill equipped we are to answer this question. As well as a great deal of uncertainty, some of the answers I have heard of what a Christian would say in this situation have not been well thought through and would not help someone make the most important decision of his life.

So how might we simply and joyfully celebrate and facilitate this moment?

A really useful starting point for answering this question is to go to the simplest of the four stories about Jesus and see what his message was to those who wanted to follow him. Mark, who tells the shortest, bluntest and most direct story of the life of Jesus, recounts that he announces his arrival with the command, 'Repent and believe the good news!'[1] Let us examine those two instructions.

Repent

One of the great advantages of the digital revolution is that we never need be bored ever again. On a portable device in our pocket we have access to an endless stream of information and entertainment. This never-ending feed of pixels is not always good for us and there have been times when I have been sitting on the toilet scrolling aimlessly down a ceaseless wall of social media, losing track of time with every thumb movement. What breaks the flow in these scenarios is an inner voice that screams sense into me and cries from the depth of my being, *'What on earth are you doing? Stop wasting your life! Turn it off!'* I then pull myself together and resolve not to succumb to my addiction to other people's news next time around. This, on the smallest of scales, is what repentance is all about. It is a radical rethinking of your life; it's the son in the pigsty who comes to his senses, it's my mate Adam lying awake all night confessing his sins to a God who heard him. It is the realization that your life has been going in the wrong direction, that you are fatally scarred with your own waywardness and brokenness and that you need a saviour to put it right. In story terms, it is the remorseful acknowledgement that there are pages, perhaps even full chapters, that you wish you could rip out of the book or redact with a black marker pen. The Greek word for repent is *metanoia*, which literally means a transformation of the heart. In repentance, we listen to the cry to stop wasting our lives, say sorry, begin the journey home and resolve to live with God at the centre of our lives.

Believe

'Trust me mate, it's deep enough,' he shouted, his mouth no more than a couple of centimetres from my ear. The pounding of waterfalls roared all around me. When I looked straight ahead from the edge of my precipice, scintillatingly beautiful scenery surrounded me. When I looked down, a tiny pool awaited my entrance a dizzying distance below. When I looked back, a giggling gaggle of mates dressed, like me, in wetsuits and brightly coloured helmets, encouraged me to take the plunge. 'What's the worst that can happen?' I knew full well that the answer to that question was death. The expert instructor stood next to me telling me that the pool was deep enough and that if I missed the protruding crag a few feet down, everything would be fine. Ultimately, the Christian faith and a relationship with the Author is about trust. And this word 'believe' sums it up. In a Western, academic culture, belief means giving your intellectual assent to, being sure in your mind that something is true. When Jesus was asking people to believe the good news, he wasn't just asking them to think of it as factual, but to trust in it in a way that affects how you live your life. The Greek word in this instance is *pisteuō*, which carries the meaning of placing your full confidence in something, which is much more than just believing something to be true. When you believe in Jesus, in this sense, you trust him with your life, and your actions begin to back that up. As well as being a decision of the mind to choose to believe that Jesus existed, lived, died and rose again, it is a decision of the will and the heart that your life will be lived in the way of Jesus, that you trust him to change you and guide you. On the cliff edge looking down at the swirling waters, the ultimate test of my trust in the instructor was not to say 'I believe you, mate', and turn and walk away, it was to jump into the unknown. Choosing to follow Jesus invites us to take that leap of faith and trust that he will catch us again and again.

Step by step

So with these things in mind, how do we help someone repent and believe?

1 Treat the moment with the tone it deserves. Choosing to follow Jesus or not is the most important decision anyone will ever make in the entirety of his or her life. There is gravity to the moment; it is not like deciding where you are going to live or even which football team to support. They are big decisions; this is bigger. Our posture should appreciate the importance of this moment. But it is also the most joyful of occasions. Heaven's champagne corks are ready to pop, angels are readily tugging at the strings of celestial party poppers. It is about to kick off in glory! Don't be too frivolous, but don't be too sombre either. Encourage your friend and tell them that what they are doing is the most amazing thing they could ever do.

2 If your friend hasn't done so already, ask them what has brought them to this moment now. If you have been journeying with someone for a while then this might not be needed, but especially if you do not know their story, this can be a helpful opportunity for them to articulate where they are coming from.

3 Explain that they simply need to:
   (a) say sorry for where they have got it wrong;
   (b) thank Jesus for dying and rising again to set them free and bring them new life;
   (c) tell God that they want to follow him for the rest of their life.

4 Encourage the person to do this in their own words, out loud, and to talk personally to God. Each time I have done this there has never been awkwardness. In the countless times I have been there at this moment, my experience is that people are excitedly desperate to talk to God and pour out how they feel.

5 Once your friend has finished, be really happy! Encourage them; say, 'Well done!' Tell them that the Bible says that a party is now happening on their behalf and assure them that, although this is the start of a new day and a new journey, nothing can now separate them from God or snatch them away from God. Pray for your friend, that they will know God is with them and will go on to make a difference in life for him.

6 Give your friend a few top tips for the first days as a Christian. These should be from personal experience rather than 'textbook answers'. Enthuse your friend with the things that you have found useful in your walk with Jesus. Explain how you pray, read the Bible, do community and what fuels your faith.

What you will often find is that people are more ready than you realize. God has been working in the background, preparing them for this moment. When Ben (Chapter 1) turned to me and said, 'Okay, I think I am ready to give my life', I went through this simple journey with him. When he prayed, I nervously wondered what he was about to say and if I would have to reiterate a few things. The reality was, as it has been almost every time, that what he prayed was way better than anything else I could have come up with. He was brutally and beautifully honest, enthusiastically and earnestly sincere and meant every word.

The chapter title, 'What must I do to be saved?', comes from an encounter that Paul and his friend Silas have with a prison guard in the book of Acts in the Bible, the early adventures of Christians. Paul and Silas are in prison for their faith, when an earthquake hits the prison. The jailer wakes up to find the prison doors open. He thinks the captives are gone and so is about to kill himself, presumably fearing the consequences of being found neglecting his duty. However, Paul and the others have not run away. They announce their presence and, when the jailer finds them he asks the Christians this famous question. In response, Paul and Silas respond with that same Greek word that Jesus used, *pisteuō*, 'believe', put all of your trust in God. In the 2,000 years since, billions have asked that question and responded to the message of Jesus by praying a simple prayer that has changed their lives and their eternal destinies. All of us need to be ready to help those who ask that question, or come to the point of decision, to make the most important step of their lives.

14
Worth it

Some discouragement

We are almost there. As we near the end of our journey together I want to fill you with hope but give you a dose of realism too. Let's begin with the spoonful of realism. Open wide . . .

Bearing your story is hard.

The road is fraught with disappointment, rejection and heartache. Looking back over the pages of this book, you will have noticed a good number of people whose stories seemingly end with a 'happily ever after'. For each of those there have been other stories that have ended 'to be continued'.

When I have preached a message of good news and offered an opportunity for people to respond, most of the time more people say 'Thanks, but no thanks' than 'Yes, please'.

When I was at university, I invited my whole corridor of twenty-four mates to Student Alpha. Twenty-two said they would come. Four came. Two left halfway through. No-one came back for the second week.

Matt, who gave his life to Jesus in the hospital waiting room, took it back again less than a year later and wouldn't call himself a Christian today.

I have a list of friends whom I pray for almost every day, some of whom have been there for a discouragingly long time.

I am reading *The Chronicles of Narnia* with Caleb at the moment. They are beautifully rich in allegory of the Christian story and the story-bearing life. As I read them to my 6-year-old there have been a couple of moments where I have struggled to get the words out because tears are rolling down my cheeks and I am choking with the emotion of what I am reading. I was very proud to hold it together for the moment when Aslan is killed on the stone table, but his resurrection was too much, prompting compassion from my son, 'Daddy, why are you crying at a book about a lion?'

My latest tearful battle has been in *Prince Caspian*, where Lucy's faith in Aslan means that for a time she is the only one who can see him. She is woken by Aslan in the middle of the night and sent by him to wake up her siblings and a doubting dwarf. She has to get them to follow her and the lion, but is told that they will not be able to see him at first for themselves.

> It's a terrible thing to have to wake four people, all older than yourself and all very tired, for the purposes of telling them something they probably won't believe and making them do something they certainly won't like. 'I mustn't think about it, I must just do it,' thought Lucy.[1]

What I tried to express to Caleb was that I was crying because at times this is how sharing faith can feel. You know you have a story. You know following Jesus is the right thing to do. If only they could see what I see. If only they knew the life of love, peace, faith, purpose and hope that was waiting for them. But getting our friends to that place can feel like waking them from a sleep they don't want to be woken from, to follow a God who is difficult to see at first – and we can feel like it all depends on us.

But the rewards are too great, the stakes too high, and at times we dig deep and say with Lucy Pevensie, 'I must just do it.'

Sharing faith is hard. But it is worth it.

Three lessons from four friends

One of my favourite encounters of Jesus is a moment when four friends bring their paralysed friend to him.[2] The house where Jesus is preaching is so full that they take some pretty drastic action, climb up on the roof, burrow their way through the ceiling and lower their mate on his bed into the middle of the place where Jesus is standing. I have a lot of questions about this. What happened to the roof rubble? Where did the men get digging implements and lowering rope from? Did they worry about dropping a man who was already paralysed? Did Jesus find the whole episode a little bit funny? Was the man whose house is now ruined compensated? Did Jesus heal that too?

What happens when the poor bloke finally gets to Jesus is wonderful. Jesus forgives his sins and tells him to walk out of the crowded room. So he does. A man who could not walk enters a building on a bed through a roof and walks out through the front door. At face value, the story is about the miraculous healing power of the Son of God, but it has some beautiful and profound lessons to teach us about evangelism. Here are a few.

First, the men who bring their paralysed friend on his mat know that his only hope is Jesus. There is no health insurance or free hospital care for him, no way of providing for his family. Many in his community would have even seen his paralysis as his or his family's fault, divine retribution for sins committed. (In another similar incident, when Jesus heals a blind man, his disciples ask him whose sinful behaviour caused his condition.) The friend is living in shame and wondering from his mat where his next meal is coming from. The script of his storyboard reads not only frustration but desperation. His future is not just a life of misery, it might not be life at all.

The chips are down. The stakes are high. This encounter really matters.

Presumably they have heard Jesus is in town. Perhaps one of them has encountered him on a previous visit to Capernaum. They will do anything to get their friend in front of Jesus. Such is their desperation that they will commit first-century criminal damage, risk humiliation, injury and even rejection from Jesus to get the guy to his feet. They know an encounter with the healer from Nazareth will be a game-changer. Sometimes our attitude in regard to our friends who don't know Jesus can be pretty indifferent. We would like them to share our world view, and they might be a bit happier if they came to church with us. I wonder what would happen if we had the same heartfelt, relentless belief that the only hope for our mates was meeting one who has changed our own lives. Bearing our story, graciously communicating the story of God and finding the connection points between these stories and those of our friends and culture is the best thing we can do for everyone we know. Like the friends in the story, we do whatever we can to bring our friends to the King. We pray, we listen, we chat, we learn our story, we invite, we love, we live differently, we lay down our lives, we struggle and strain and dig holes in whatever obstacles stand in our way to give them a chance.

Second, it is not just one person who brings his paralysed friend to the house. The friends already go to great lengths, but can you imagine what it would have been like had it been just one of them? In our individualistic culture, and especially when we may be the only Christian our friend knows, sharing faith can feel so lonely, as though we are carrying our mates over our shoulders to Jesus on our own. Don't be a lone ranger. Find ways of involving others. One of the best things you can do is find like-minded others who will pray for you, pray with you, cheer you on, with whom you can share encouragements and disappointments along the way. If at all possible, take opportunities to introduce your non-Christian friends to your Christian ones. Meeting other Jesus followers will help them see the common difference he makes in their lives too. Evangelism is a collaborative effort, not a solo sport.

Third, the effort is worth it. The Bible text doesn't record the moment, but I would love to have seen the reaction of the friends. Presumably they are still on the roof, their necks straining through the cavity, their eyes fixed on the encounter. Maybe there is only room enough for one head, so he is reporting back to the others. Imagine what it was like for them when Jesus tells their mate to pick up his mat and walk, and he does! Aside from the relief of not having to repeat the journey as a makeshift ambulance, every ounce of desperation turns to joy. Picture them rushing off the house roof to be reunited with their now mobile friend. It was worth it! As I think about the moments in my life that have meant the most, it has been those when I have been involved in the pivotal, life-changing moments of others that move me the most and of which I am most proud. When I reach the end of my days and ponder the significance of my life, it will be individual lives that I have seen turn towards Jesus that I look at and remind myself that God used me. I will think of Adam, and hopefully by that time many more, and will be grateful.

Albert

I am here today because of a man called Albert McMackin. Albert was like the men in the story. He had a friend he was desperate to bring to Jesus. His name was William. Albert knew there was a preacher coming to his town and, ready to take any opportunity to get his mate to hear the good news, Albert invited him along. William declined, but Albert persisted. Eventually, Albert said he would let William drive the bus (something he loved to do) if he agreed to come. At the very last opportunity, William drove the bus to the meeting and hung around on the edge of the gathering. When he heard the message about who Jesus is, his need to be forgiven and know God, he decided to become a Christian. Not long after doing so, his life so dramatically transformed, William decided to become a preacher himself. He was quite good at it.

William is better known as Billy Graham.

William Franklin Graham Jr has spoken to more people than anyone else in history. A staggering 2.2 billion people heard about

Jesus through his talks. He spoke to over 215 million people live from stages in countries all over the world. At his meetings, 2.2 million of these made decisions to follow Jesus.[3]

One of those was my dad. He told me that a pivotal moment in his story was responding at a Billy Graham event.

Then, when I was a little boy, my dad told me about Jesus. I am here because of Albert McMackin.

Billy Graham was also catalytic in starting Youth for Christ. In 1946 he was so moved by the need to reach young people in Britain that British Youth for Christ was established. When I finished my law degree, it was YFC who took a chance on me, invested in me and gave me the opportunity to share good news with young people. I am here because of Albert McMackin.

Millions have heard of William. Not many know about Albert. We can't all be a Billy Graham. We can all be his friend who will not give up on him and will let him drive the bus.

Put yourself for a moment in the shoes of Albert in 1934. He was not thinking of me, my dad or any of the billions who would be influenced by his mate William. All he cared about was his friend knowing Jesus. He was like the four friends carrying the invalid on the mat. Now put yourself in his shoes years later, turning on the television to see the man he led to Jesus preaching to crowds of tens of thousands. Imagine his smile and sense of pride in the impact of his actions. Whatever the stresses were in trying to help Billy, however many awkward moments, whoever else he was rejected by and whatever disappointments he carried, he would say in the end it was worth it.

And that is how it is as a story bearer. It takes practice and determination to craft and remember your story.

It is worth it.

It takes commitment and hard work to learn and delight in God's story.

It is worth it.

It takes a lifetime of perseverance and frequent disappointment to pray regularly for friends to know Jesus.

It is worth it.

True friendship is costly and demanding in a full and frantic life.

It is worth it.

You were created to bear your story, to live it and tell it to bring hope and life and invite others to take their place in the greatest story ever told. When you play a part in someone's journey to faith it is a beautiful and wonderful moment. Knowing Jesus is not just a nice added extra to enhance our lives that little bit more, like a revolutionary new app; it is the core of all that we need, the connection our hearts have been craving for from their first beat.

Dave

Dave is one of my best mates. We've all got a mate called Dave. I met Dave in the first week at university. He is one of the warmest, most caring people I know. Life is real, fun and beautiful when you are around Dave. And I have been praying for him to know Jesus for over ten years.

A few years ago, Dave was navigating a challenging situation in his life, talking about the need to get away from it all, and so we invited him to come on holiday with us as a family. The main purpose of the time away was to help him switch off from what was going on back home, and we had a lot of fun touring distilleries, playing beach cricket and fishing. But he also spent time reflecting on his life situation, and one day, while out playing golf, Dave poured his heart out to me and asked for my advice. I sat there thinking for a while, and had honestly reached the end of my human wisdom. The situation he found himself in was extremely compli-cated. I said, not very pastorally, 'Mate, your life is a bit of a mess, I just don't know . . .' We both saw the funny side of my less than compassionate answer before I gave the only advice I could think of: 'Dave, I think the only thing you can do is give your life to Jesus and let him sort it out.'

In this second I honestly prayed hard and wondered if this was the moment, like so many I have described in this book. I imagined he would turn to me and say, 'What must I do to be saved?' He didn't. Instead, he said some words that were as profound as they were hilarious: 'What's the second-best option?'

More recently, I was preaching on a Sunday evening in Newcastle where Dave lives and so I arranged to stay with him the night before. In the preceding week, I got a text from him that almost made me fall off my chair.

'Would you like to come to church with me on Sunday morning?'

I texted back and explained he had got it the wrong way round. Normally it was the Christian who invited the non-Christian to church! He explained that a friend of his was leading the service and he was going along for moral support. So that Sunday the two of us sat in the balcony and cheered on his mate. The strange thing was that I didn't know many of the songs, which is weird for a 'professional Christian'. But after a couple of hymns, the words to 'Amazing Grace' came on the screen:

Amazing Grace, how sweet the sound
That saved a wretch like me!
I once was lost, but now am found,
Was blind, but now I see.[4]

These words communicate the core of the gospel message. They speak of the beauty, majesty and mystery of what Jesus has done for us. They tell the story of all of us who know him, that once we were broken, lost and unknowing of the greatest love in the universe, but now we have been undeservedly restored, rescued, welcomed home and had our eyes opened to relentless affection and a life beyond our wildest imaginations. Needless to say, when I sing 'Amazing Grace' I do so with a little gusto.

This Sunday was no exception and, having mumbled my way through a few tunes I was unfamiliar with, I sang 'Amazing Grace' with a significant amount of enthusiasm. My volume, coupled with a lack of self-consciousness, meant that my efforts were noticed by more than a few people in the pews below, some of whom turned round to see who was making all the noise.

A couple of weeks later I was on the phone to Dave and we laughed as we recalled the incident. Better still, he had an update. 'Phil, I went back to that church we went to . . . they're still talking about your singing.' I was flattered. But not missing an opportunity to tell Dave a little bit more about Jesus, I asked him if I could explain why I belted out the lyrics in the manner that I did. I told him again what the song meant to me, and in an exasperated attempt to articulate how amazing the grace was, I decided to rewrite the song as if it were just 'Average Grace'. It went something like this:

Average Grace, how bland the sound
That slightly improved my life.
I went to church and like the songs,
And now I have to be nice.

The truth is that grace is anything but average. C. S. Lewis said, 'Christianity is a statement which, if false, is of *no* importance, and, if true, of infinite importance. The one thing it cannot be is moderately important.'[5] We must never get to the point where we consider the message of Jesus to be an average upgrade. He is worth more than being treated like an extra GB of data to a phone contract or heated seats in a car. We must never diminish our story to one that invites a shrug of moderate indifference. If we lower the stakes, we do God, ourselves and our friends a disservice.

It is good news, not good advice.

Jesus changes everything.

I long for Dave to stop living in 'the second-best option'. He is, at the time of writing, still on a journey, but I am full of hope that one day he will belt out 'Amazing Grace' with even more gusto than me.

Go for it

I am full of hope for you, that as you have read this book you have become increasingly aware of the weight and power of the story that you bear. I pray that you have been inspired to draw others closer to the Author and encouraged to realize that the task is not as awkward or as daunting as you might have once thought. I hope that you have taken seriously the tasks of learning your story and the story of God, and have committed to listening well to others' stories and that of the culture you find yourself in. I hope that you have been challenged and inspired to pray more for your friends who don't know Jesus yet and to throw yourself again into deeper friendships with them and the God who created you.

The Author of the greatest story of all is still writing. As the plot of history unfolds, how will your life have lived out the narrative? When the last page is turned and the screen fades to black, may you be able to say that you have played your part well. May your legacy be that you prayed, loved and invited many others into the adventure. The Author is looking for co-writers to help him tell the tale of history. Will you bear your story? Will you tell it well?

So reach for your settings and turn your 'li-fi' on.
Because the Author is still speaking.
His heart is still beating.
And the story is love and with it he frees us.
Because the Author has a name and his name is Jesus.

The Evangelical Alliance

evangelical alliance
together making Jesus known

The Evangelical Alliance is made up of hundreds of organizations, thousands of churches and tens of thousands of individuals, joined together for the sake of the gospel. Representing our members since 1846, the Evangelical Alliance is the oldest and largest evangelical unity movement in the UK.

United in mission and voice, we exist to serve and strengthen the work of the church in our communities and throughout society. Highlighting the significant opportunities and challenges facing the church today, we work together to resource Christians so that they are able to act upon their faith in Jesus, to speak up for the gospel, justice and freedom in their areas of influence.

Working across the UK, with offices in London, Cardiff, Glasgow and Belfast, our members come together from across denominations, locations, age groups and ethnicities, all sharing a passion to know Jesus and make him known.

Notes

Preface

1 Luke 15:7.

Introduction: There is a story to be told

1 Quoted in R. Brand, *Revolution* (Random House, London, 2015), p. 37.
2 Romans 8:19–23.
3 I am grateful for the influence of Roy Crowne and Bill Muir, who passionately articulate story-based evangelism in R. Crowne and B. Muir, *The Art of Connecting* (Authentic, Milton Keynes, 2003).

1 Story bearers

1 2 Corinthians 5:17.

2 Contagious

1 See <https://www.bbc.co.uk/news/av/uk-36261996/guy-goma-bbc-s-best-worst-interview>.
2 K. DeYoung, *Crazy Busy* (Crossway, Wheaton IL, 2013), p. 16.

3 The power of story

1 D. Miller, *Building a Story Brand* (HarperCollins, London, 2017), p. 15.
2 C. Gallo, *The Storyteller's Secret: From TED Speakers to Business Legends. Why Some Ideas Catch On and Others Don't* (St Martin's Press, New York, 2016).
3 C. Gallo, *Talk Like Ted* (St Martin's Press, New York, 2014).

4 S. Hipps, *Flickering Pixels: How Technology Shapes Your Faith* (Zondervan, Grand Rapids MI, 2009), p. 68.
5 See <https://en.wikipedia.org/wiki/Wikipedia:Size_of_ Wikipedia>.
6 D. Siegel, *Brainstorm: The Power and Purpose of the Teenage Brain* (Penguin, New York, 2013), pp. 171–5.
7 P. Smith, *Lead with a Story: A Guide to Crafting Business Narratives that Captivate, Convince and Inspire* (Amacom Books, New York, 2012).

4 God's story

1 G. Kelly, *Church Actually* (Monarch, London, 2012).
2 A quote accredited to Canadian pastor Oswald J. Smith.
3 Judges 2:10.
4 J. McDowell, *Evidence that Demands a Verdict* (Campus Crusade for Christ, San Bernardino CA, 1972), p. 167.
5 J. A. Francis, *One Solitary Life* (1963), pp. 1–7.
6 NB – a mixed grill still works without the steak. This metaphor only works if you place the same extreme level of emphasis on the steak that I do. In my opinion, a mixed grill without a steak is pointless, futile and belongs in the bin.

5 Telling God's story

1 L. Sweet, *The Well-Played Life: Why Pleasing God Doesn't Have to Be Such Hard Work* (Tyndale Momentum, Carol Stream IL, 2014), p. 193.
2 At this stage, if you still have a Nokia 3210 or you are listening to the dial tone of your home phone you will have to abandon the analogy – it's a smartphone exclusive.
3 Agape, *Knowing God Personally* (Agape Ministries, Birmingham, 1995).
4 1 John 4:7–21; Psalm 139; Genesis 1:27–31.
5 Luke 15:11–16; Romans 3:23; 6:23; Genesis 3.

6 Romans 5:8; Luke 15:20–24; Colossians 1:15–23.

7 Ephesians 2:8–9; 2 Corinthians 5:17; Revelation 7:15–17.

6 Your story

1 Galatians 2:20.

2 MSN Messenger is to WhatsApp what VHS is to Netflix. Google these terms if necessary.

3 1 Peter 3:15.

4 Psalm 34:18.

5 Philip Collins expands on this historical moment in great detail in P. Collins, *When They Go Low, We Go High: Speeches that Shape the World – and Why We Need Them* (HarperCollins, London, 2018).

6 T. Suttle and S. McKnight, *Shrink: Faithful Ministry in a Church-Growth Culture* (Zondervan, Grand Rapids MI, 2014).

7 Living your story

1 Matthew 5:13.

2 K. Heaseman, *Evangelicals in Action: An Appraisal of Their Social Work in the Victorian Era* (Geoffrey Bles, London, 1962), pp. 13–14.

3 <www.streetpastors.org/>.

4 <https://capuk.org/>.

5 <www.trusselltrust.org/>.

6 <www.cinnamonnetwork.co.uk/wp-content/uploads/2015/05/Final-National-Report.pdf>.

7 2 Corinthians 3:2–3.

8 <https://millennial-leader.com/>.

9 Proverbs 24:16.

8 Stories to hear

1 <www.ted.com/talks/ernesto_sirolli_want_to_help_someone_shut_up_and_listen/transcript#t-171918>.

2 D. Miller, *Building a Story Brand* (HarperCollins, London, 2017), p. ix.

3 John 5:17.

4 John 5:19.

5 D. Bannatyne, *Anyone Can Do It: My Story* (Orion, London, 2007), p. 231.

6 D. Carnegie, *How to Win Friends and Influence People* (Simon & Schuster, New York, 1936).

7 Proverbs 1:5.

8 John 10:10.

9 John 1:12.

9 Read the signs of the times

1 John 7:37–38.

2 Mark 12:17.

3 Genesis 1:26.

4 Acts 17:22.

5 1 Chronicles 12:32.

6 T. Elmore, *Generation iY: Our Last Chance to Save Their Future* (Poet Gardening Publishing, Atlanta GA, 2010).

7 <www.pewresearch.org/wp-content/uploads/sites/3/2010/10/millennials-confident-connected-open-to-change.pdf>.

8 <https://eu.usatoday.com/story/news/nation/2013/06/03/online-dating-marriage/2377961/>.

9 <http://techland.time.com/2011/05/27/study-53-of-youngsters-would-choose-technology-over-sense-of-smell/>.

10 Matthew E. Brashears, Miller McPherson, Lynn Smith-Lovin (June 2006), 'Social Isolation in America', *American Sociological Review*, 71: 353–375.

11 A. Alter, *Irresistible* (Vintage, London, 2017), p. 109.

12 N. Carr, *The Shallows* (Atlantic, London, 2010), p. 7.

13 <https://yfc.co.uk/rethinkingculture/>.

14 <www.bbc.co.uk/news/newsbeat-43485581>.

15 <www.churchofengland.org/sites/default/files/2017-11/Dr%20 Rachel%20Jordan-Wolf%20-%20Talking%20Jesus%20Youth.pdf >.

16 <http://talkingjesus.org/2015-research/>.

17 <www.bbc.co.uk/news/uk-45679730?fbclid=IwAR1VIvpQPDVJh mDfKdwoONhKxHnTFQqn2oIXqMhzJPlOnnyrsdDd7y_lhAw>.

18 <www.youtube.com/watch?v=Xaq4nN2QwEI>.

10 Drawing the threads together

1 T. Suttle and S. McKnight, *Shrink: Faithful Ministry in a Church-Growth Culture* (Zondervan, Grand Rapids MI, 2014).

2 Hebrews 12:3 (MSG).

3 Micah 6:8.

4 Romans 5:5.

5 Psalm 68:5.

6 Lamentations 3:22–23.

7 Acts 8:30.

8 Acts 8:35.

11 Weaving in the other stories

1 John 15:15.

2 John 15:13.

3 John 13:35.

4 Job 2:13.

5 L. Sweet, *So Beautiful: Divine Design for Life and Church* (David C. Cook, Colorado Springs, 2009).

6 John 19:26–27.

12 Tightening the cords

1 1 Corinthians 3:6.

2 Acts 16:14.

3 1 Corinthians 12:3.

4 T. Keller, *Prayer: Experiencing Awe and Intimacy with God* (Hodder & Stoughton, London, 2016).

5 1 Timothy 2:1–6.
6 Matthew 6:10.
7 Colossians 4:2–3.
8 Ephesians 6:19.
9 Colossians 4:5.
10 <www.youtube.com/watch?v=UXyZHYsVkoI>.

13 What must I do to be saved?

1 Mark 1:15.

14 Worth it

1 C. S. Lewis, *Prince Caspian* (HarperCollins, New York, 1951), p. 126.
2 Mark 2:1–12.
3 https://factsandtrends.net/2018/02/21/billy-grahams-life-ministry-by-the-numbers/>.
4 'Amazing Grace' was written by the English poet John Newton (1725–1807).
5 C. S. Lewis, 'Christian Apologetics', in *God in the Dock* (Eerdmans, Grand Rapids MI, 1970), p. 101; emphasis in original.